ENRICHING AND EXTENDING THE NATIONAL CURRICULUM

Kogan Page Books for Teachers series
Series Editor: Tom Marjoram

ENRICHING AND EXTENDING THE NATIONAL CURRICULUM

Deborah Eyre and Tom Marjoram

Books for Teachers
Series Editor: Tom Marjoram

KOGAN PAGE

First published in 1990 by Kogan Page Ltd
120 Pentonville Road, London N1 9JN

Typeset by DP Photosetting, Aylesbury, Bucks
Printed and bound by Biddles Ltd, Guildford

British Library Cataloguing in Publication Data
A CIP catalogue record for this book is
available from the British Library.

ISBN 0–7494–0147–8

Contents

Introduction

The National Curriculum prescribes a minimum educational diet for nearly all children aged 5–16, in all maintained schools, of three core subjects – English, mathematics and science – and seven foundation subjects – history, geography, technology, art, music, PE, and a modern language from the age of 11. RE must also be part of the package.

Attainment targets (ATs) and programmes of study for ten different levels in four of these subjects have already been published; others will follow later. It is assumed that most children will reach level 6 or 7 in most attainment targets of most subjects by the age of 16. Thus, the Education Reform Act 1988 implicitly recognises that there are able and even highly gifted pupils in schools who may attain levels 8, 9 or 10. Apart from this, however, there is little *explicit* cognisance of the widely varying abilities, needs and interests of children in our schools. The contents of, say, level x for attainment target y in subject z are the same for all and there is no guidance as to how these contents might be enriched, elaborated and extended for the very ablest or adapted for the less able.

That the Act neither lays down criteria about method, approach or timing nor forbids the teaching of other material or even other subjects is one of its virtues. Thus, it will be the job of the teacher to modify, enrich and extend the curriculum according to individual needs and to provide additional challenges for those who are capable of assimilating a wider and heavier work load.

In the first five chapters of this book we discuss the processes of enrichment and extension and why, when and how these may be applied to the basic programme.

Chapter 6 deals with people and organisations who can provide the means and extra ideas and resources necessary. Chapter 7 gives some examples of existing good school practice and personal experiences

7

while Chapters 8 and 9 list respectively external organisations, societies and institutions that offer help, and resources and projects already available. An extensive bibliography is provided at the end of the book.

Our book does not make a plea for perpetual enrichment or continuous extension, nor does it suggest that the National Curriculum programmes are deficient or too meagre for basic educational health. On the contrary, the entitlement for every child bestowed by the 1988 Act is broader, more balanced and more relevant than some received before. Nevertheless, within that broad provision there must be and indeed is scope for differential treatment to suit the widely varying needs that all pupils experience from time to time.

The National Curriculum should not be seen as a strait-jacket limiting choice but rather like the sonnet, sonata and symphonic forms within which so much freedom and creativity is possible. It should be regarded as a comparable learning structure or set of guidelines within which the scope for experiment, innovation and advance is increased.

This book is not a new approach to education developed by its authors, but rather an attempt to draw together and explain the good practice already found in many schools. Enrichment and extension, as a method of meeting the needs of the individual, is supported in Britain by the National Association for Curriculum Enrichment and Extension (NACE) and the authors would like to express their thanks to all members of that Association whose ideas and views have contributed to this book. We would particularly like to thank Mike Deans and Oxfordshire colleagues Sue McMillan, Sylvia Jordon, Richard Arrowsmith and Ann Wilson; also Johanna Raffan (chairman of NACE) for her interest and support and Julian Whybra (Essex LEA) for supplying such a comprehensive list of materials.

Finally, this book would not have reached the publishers without the excellent work of Janice Blackburn, our secretary. She not only produced impressive copy and layout but also dealt with the problem of working with two authors, living 100 miles apart, with unfailing good humour and tolerance. Our thanks, Janice.

Deborah Eyre
Tom Marjoram

Chapter 1

Why Enrich and/or Extend the Curriculum?

Definitions

One dictionary definition of 'enrich' is 'to make rich, to fertilize, to adorn, to enhance'. Perhaps the most helpful of these verbs in the educational sense are the second and fourth. In this book we shall be thinking of *curriculum enrichment* as a process by which school work becomes alive and exciting and by which learning is an organic, growing, never-ending but ever fascinating journey. It is not about the perfunctory completion of routine tasks but about enlarging horizons, tackling problems whose solutions give rise to further problems, seeking peaks, experimenting with new materials, processes and ideas. It is also about enhancing the quality of life in the classroom and heightening sensitivity.

The same dictionary offers the meaning of 'extend' as 'to stretch out, prolong in any direction, to enlarge, expand, to widen, to hold out, bestow or impart'. And certainly we can recognise a sense of *curriculum extension* as a reaching ahead, or going beyond what is required, or searching for the new.

The terms enrichment and extension overlap and are sometimes used interchangeably, even synonymously. Dickens' lovable character, Sam Weller, besides being a store of pithy epigrams, 'had a knowledge of London that was *extensive* and peculiar' which carries overtones of richness as well as extent. In this book, however, we seek to distinguish between the two and their different aims and functions in the classroom.

This first chapter discusses the rationale of curriculum enrichment and/or extension.

The National Curriculum

From September 1989 all maintained primary and secondary schools in England and Wales had to provide, for all children between 5 and 16, a national curriculum of religious education and nine other *foundation* subjects – English, mathematics, science, technology, history, geography, art, music and physical education, the first three being *core subjects*. To these were to be added, for children of secondary school age only, a modern foreign language.

Working parties in all these subjects are being set up and, indeed, in each of the core subjects we now have a description of the ten levels of attainment through which pupils may progress between 5 and 16.

Reports on all these subjects make it clear that not all pupils will reach level 10 by the age of 16. Indeed, the least able may only reach level 4 in some subjects. Only a few will reach level 10. Most will reach level 6 or 7.

Professor Brian Start of Melbourne University in a Keynote Address, 'The Tyranny of Age' delivered to the World Conference on Gifted and Talented Children in Sydney in July 1989, produced some startling research findings.

Children of IQ	25		50	75	and 100, for example,
learn at speeds	V (The rate of acquiring facts)		1½V,	2V	and 4V

Thus, although in a mixed ability class we may well find two pupils of IQ 75 and 100, the first will get through the curriculum in *half* the time of the second. Yet there they are, marching up the school in lock step because it is deemed necessary to keep pupils together by *age* group. This form of classification is not used anywhere else in society. Moreover, emotional development is more closely tied to IQ than to chronology, so there are also liable to be, in the same class, mismatches of feeling, sensitivity and aesthetic development.

The new National Curriculum does at least recognise the great differences of attainment to be expected at the same age; it also makes provision for the very able in levels 9 and 10.

It does not, cannot and should not describe *in great detail* what constitutes a particular level of attainment. Thus, for example, under mathematics level 2 'shape and space' we read, 'Recognising squares, rectangles, circles, triangles, cubes, cuboids and spheres and talking about them. Understanding turning through right angles. Recognising types of movement: straight (translation), turning (rotation) and flip (reflection).'

This, like so many other level descriptions, begs many questions which will be answered in very different ways by different teachers and

Figure 1.1: *Recognising squares*

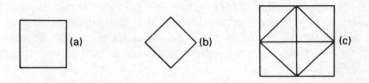

'National Curriculum textbook' writers.

'Recognising squares' requires closer definition. Many children readily see that (a) in Figure 1.1 above is a square but would call (b) a 'diamond'.

Asked how many squares there were in (c) they would probably produce various answers such as 1, 4, 5 or 6. It might take a 'level 10 child' to recognise that the number of squares on a chess board is not 64 but 204. In the same way 'understanding turning' is a statement which can vary from the rudimentary to the sophisticated.

The commentary surrounding the introduction of the National Curriculum seems to agree that each level description is to be read in an elementary sense. It has been jokingly labelled 'the BBC' – 'Baker's Basic Curriculum' or the 'Broad Basic Curriculum'. In other words, it describes *minimum competencies* at each level. Schools and teachers must feel free to *augment, enrich and extend* the curriculum in its whole as well as its parts. The Act does not forbid secondary or primary pupils for that matter from studying two or three foreign languages. It does not proscribe Greek or philosophy or subjects not listed. It is concerned with minimum educational entitlements for all children while leaving doors open for enrichment and extension of all kinds. Indeed, the Act does not insist upon chronological age grouping and so we may find schools coping with level differentiation problems in new ways.

On the other hand, as the examples in Figure 1.1 hint, pupils in the same class, at the same national level, learning about squares could be working together, but individually, on a very wide variety of problems about squares. Indeed, in small country schools pupils of widely differing ability – and age – have always had to be taught together. Our book discusses primarily this and other curriculum differentiation problems.

GCSE examinations

The new GCSE examinations also allow a wider range of 'target' than was possible at GCE. But more importantly, they afford a much wider range of response. Thus, in some subjects a substantial proportion of marks may be obtained for practical work. In mathematics, pupils may offer extended pieces of mathematical investigation as part of their examination work. In music, candidates must display an ability to perform, compose and criticise as well as answering theoretical questions.

This new examination scene, which could well influence A/S, A level and other school examinations, clearly adds another argument for the need to enrich and extend further the basic classroom curriculum.

Integration

Since the publication of the Warnock Report in 1978 and similar documents to the Fish Report on ILEA (1985), schools have been integrating more and more children with handicaps and learning difficulties into mainstream classes. Indeed, another book in the Kogan Page Books for Teachers series (*Towards Integration: Special Needs in an Ordinary School* by Christine Gilbert and Michael Hart) describes a remarkable experiment and notable achievement in this field.

The implications of the trend towards integration are many. Schools with such children require a much wider variety of materials, equipment and methodologies than before. They may also require technological aids such as modified computer keyboards, radio links, wheelchair ramps, enhanced visual displays and so on. They certainly also need increased capacity to enrich and extend the basic National Curriculum. For some children exemption clauses may have to be invoked necessitating a *modified* curriculum which may also need to be enriched and extended.

Presentation

When the author of this chapter was at primary school, a magic lantern show was a great treat. Indeed, at secondary school, the geography master had only to remove the dust cover from the epidiascope for some pupils to wake up and quiver with expectation.

Nowadays, our children are subjected to an unremitting barrage of sounds and images. Walkman sets are *de rigueur*. I have even met pupils who seem unable to concentrate in silence or do homework without the radio on.

Only in school do we still hear the squeak of chalk on board. One would certainly not suggest for a minute that the TV/video/pop stream should now invade our schools and take over from teachers but one wonders whether we have learned enough from the input and influence of the media to pep up our own classroom approaches. Enrichment and extension is not simply about content but also skills.

There are certainly more keyboards, cameras, videos in school than at one time but the predominant communication modes in school are still speech and handwriting. Students generally are not taught to type, use word processors, operate computers, cameras or video cameras. Work could often be far better presented, edited and illustrated. Desktop publishing techniques have reached few schools.

Some school libraries have evolved beyond the book collection stage and now house tapes, slides, videos, facsimile documents, maps and plans, etc. Some schools do pay attention to reference and research skills, but they are the exception. In our modern media world all this hard/software and skills training should underpin the school work and learning of all children. Certainly, there are opportunities galore to enrich and extend the presentation of the curriculum. There are even opportunities to improve the basic traditional skills of reading and writing. The work of the Assessment of Performance Unit (APU) has shown us that these activites are simply headings for complexes of subskills.

Progress in reading, for example, involves basic word recognition, comprehension, comparison and inference skills. By the secondary stage some schools assume that the pupils can read and that no further reading skills need to be taught. But how many secondary school pupils can actually analyse and compare two different accounts of the same event, two different poems on the same theme, two different receipes or sets of instruction for the same task? How many can spot internal contradictions, *non sequiturs*, question-begging statements, circular arguments? How many can skim or rapid-read to get the gist of a piece of work? How many can depth-read a very complex sentence, a highly condensed verse line or a complex mathematical argument?

We referred earlier to editing as a writing skill. Too often the demands of a packed syllabus or the shortage of time mean that there is seldom opportunity to shape, polish and improve a piece of writing. It is not always possible to pen a good paraphrase or a precise précis at the first attempt. Indeed, some students have not learned to acquire a sufficiently self-critical habit to see that their writing can be improved. Lest I hoist myself with my own petard, let me hasten to admit that this is a life-long lesson which I am still learning – but it is one which should start early in the primary school. /*inconsistencies*

Such skill-sharpening is not found in all schools. Where it is it forms a very positive part of enrichment and extension of the curriculum.

Delivery

Although the previous section may appear too demanding or critical of the overworked teacher in the normal school classroom it was not so intended.

Enrichment and extension are not processes to which any given child should be *continuously* subjected. Where a child receives all the elements of the National Curriculum as decreed by law and detailed in the Curriculum Proposal documents in mathematics, science, English and those in history and other foundation areas yet to come, such a programme will add up to a very substantial and useful education. It is undoubtedly *broad*. For most children it will constitute a *balanced education and*, if well taught and practically illustrated, much of it could be more *relevant* than what was purveyed before. Seen as a whole it will not, for some children, require additions, extension or great elaboration.

We must also realise that to some extent enrichment and extension are relative terms. The 'normal' pace of work in some schools and classes would be seen as rapid in others. The 'normal' approach of the history teacher whose room is an Aladdin's cave and whose lessons are exciting and well illustrated by slides and artefacts may seem 'enriched' to other students whose work is a thorough but dreary trudge through the history textbook.

The main point, however, is to understand the *need* to enrich or extend: to *differentiate* the curriculum as occasion demands.

Few children, even the ablest, will thrive on a constant diet of over-rich food. They need time to digest. Likewise, in the classroom, a bout of enriched work and exciting challenge must often be followed by a period of free-wheeling reflection and consolidation. The internalisation of new concepts, as Vygotsky stressed, requires time and tranquillity. Often a brand-new skill requires routine repetition and practice before it can be deployed with confidence.

Similarly, few children benefit from being rushed ahead of their fellows all the time. We talk of extending and stretching the able pupils as though they were victims of some inquisitor's rack. We all need time to stand and stare, to switch off, even to take a complete rest.

Moreover, we must remember that few children grow steadily and uniformly. Many grow in fits and starts. As the pre-Plowden research showed there are indeed distinct periods of rapid growth after birth, in the early years of schooling, at menarche and puberty, in all children. This applies as much to physical as to social, emotional and intellectual growth. We can all think of our own children or our pupils or children we know who passed through periods of sparkling growth and achievement followed by plateaux and even setbacks.

Yehudi Menuhin relates how, as a young prodigy, he *intuitively* learned his violin skills and repertoire with great facility but that in adolescence, when he began to think *objectively* about his playing and the rationale behind his interpretations, he went through a period of anxiety and apparent stagnation as an artist. This phenomenon is not uncommon among performers in sport and the arts but it can also happen on a small scale with lots of ordinary pupils.

Thus, the very ablest do not develop their gifts at a uniform rate and may pass through periods when they need stimulus or challenge, periods when they need to be left alone, and periods when they need counsel, support and even remedial help.

Moreover, the gifted child is not necessarily – or even commonly – gifted or even capable in all subjects. Thus, a child may require challenge and enrichment in his or her strong subject but quite different help and support in others. An outstanding example of this was the gifted 11-year-old mathematician who read mathematics with the sixth-formers but took most of his other lessons with his contemporaries. At field sports he was notably timid and inept and required very sympathetic support.

It is also unwise to assume that certain types of pupil require enrichment while other types require extension. The fact is that the same pupil may, over the same period, be better advised to remain with a topic and pursue it in greater depth and detail than the other pupils in the class. At another period he or she may need to storm ahead and move on to more difficult texts, next year's work, or even work with older children.

In all this it is easy to think only of pupils' enrichment and challenge, disregard the teacher's own needs, and to forget that in good schools *everyone* is learning.

To differentiate the curriculum of work in such a way as to meet the very differing needs of children in a class or set or school is an exciting business. It highlights the difference between the teacher and the instructor. Some of the best forms of enrichment reside not in extra materials, new books or trips, but in the sheer quality of relationship or discipleship between teacher and taught. I recall, for example, a keen amateur archaeologist who, as an out-of-school treat, took some of his

15

class to see a real Humberbank Roman dig. Such was the interest generated and the subsequent level of work produced that it reached the attention of the national media, and a famous archaeologist, Professor Glyn Daniel, who declared it to be of serious research standard.

Another case was that of an art teacher whom I knew to be a fine painter in his own right. I persuaded him to make a habit of painting in his school art room and to let the pupils see him at work and discuss his work. The enriching effect of this was quite dramatic and markedly lifted the general level of response and the particular efforts of two quite talented pupils.

It is worth remembering that sometimes pupils have interests which they are reluctant to bring into school. One of the most successful 'Expanding Classroom' films a few years ago showed what could flow from two pupils' private interest in why petrol and oil make rainbow patterns on puddles. The teacher, Jim Rose, later chief HMI for Primary Education at the DES, and his pupils let that one question lead them forward into a whole term of rich investigational work.

Strategies

There are thus many cogent arguments for differentiating the curriculum and many reasons and occasions for, and methods of, enriching and extending it. Strategies that may be employed include *material*, *organisational* and *pedagogical* ones.

Material strategies include the provision of further reading material, extra source material of all kinds to facilitate deeper and more detailed study of the theme in hand, individual learning packs or assignment sheets such as 'Jackdaws', SMILE (Secondary Mathematics Individual Learning Experiment) and KMP (Kent Mathematics Project) mathematics materials.

Organisational provision to enrich or extend the curriculum may include extra/individual or group help *in situ* by a visiting teacher; withdrawal from the normal class to take part in a quite different activity (see PEAC (Provision for Exceptionally Able Children) classes in Western Australia, and similar); promotion for part or whole of the week regularly/occasionally to work with a more advanced class; removal to a different 'special' or more suitable school; weekend or vacation courses and workshops of the kind organised in Israel and by organisations such as the National Association for Gifted Children (NAGC) in England, visits *to* exhibitions, museums, field centres and similar locations; visits (long or short) *by* poets, painters, sculptors, explorers and the like.

Pedagogical provision lies at the heart of enrichment and extension. It represents the personal element upon which all depends. The inspirational mentor, the gifted teacher, can offer more than any amount of inanimate material and organisation. It is not without significance that the central element in Oxbridge and Dunelm is the tutorial system, or that MENSA, so long simply a society for people with high IQs, has now turned its attention to providing mentors for highly talented children.

But, however gifted the teacher, the sheer volume of work now entailed in the National Curriculum and assessment, and the need to differentiate and render viable that system, is formidable. Resources, inservice training and time will be essential. In Chapter 5 we discuss in detail the actual strategies and tactics for providing enrichment and extension in all subjects which have already been, or might in the future be, tried. A few more enterprising education authorities have encouraged the production of enrichment materials or kits for able pupils. Details of these are given in Chapter 9.

Most of the curriculum enrichment material to date has been directed towards the needs of the able rather than towards the problems of *differentiating* the curriculum for a wider variety of purposes. Good recent examples of the latter have been produced by the Hampshire Curriculum Differentiation Initiative and in Queensland by a collection of papers and guidelines entitled 'Strategies for Enrichment'.

We now consider in Chapters 2 and 3 the separate processes of enrichment and extension in greater detail.

Chapter 2
What is Enrichment?

Enrichment is any type of activity or learning which is outside the core of learning which most children undertake. Therefore, what may be termed enrichment varies from school to school, class to class and child to child. In a very lively classroom enrichment activities may be constantly available whereas in a more closely constrained environment they may only be made available for limited periods or in some cases not at all.

Enrichment refers not only to additional types of activity which may be undertaken but also to the introduction of new methods for approaching work. So, for example, a child may be given a problem-solving exercise as an enrichment activity and this may well be with a view to learning a new technique, ie problem-solving, rather than, or in addition to, a new subject. Possible areas of enrichment are unlimited: a child may learn a new language, develop a hobby, be introduced to totally new concepts such as algebra, or a new skill such as mapping. What is important is that the activities should be at an appropriate level in terms of ability and interest for the child or children involved and that enrichment should be an occasional undertaking not a day-to-day activity. A supplement to, not a replacement for, the generally recognised body of work undertaken in schools.

It may be necessary to provide an intensive programme of enrichment in particular circumstances, for example for a child returning after illness or joining school in mid-term, but generally, enrichment should be sufficiently flexible to allow children to become involved as and when they show inclination. Some children need and respond to enrichment challenge more than others. A child may show a sustained interest in one task or subject but little interest in another. Sometimes it takes a really exciting challenge to interest a child in enrichment at all – some children prefer to operate at average class level where they have the safety of knowing they are likely to find the work straightforward. Some children work slowly and will never encounter enrichment if it is dependent on finishing other work first. Therefore, enrichment needs to fit the children and the circumstances for which it is intended.

Why do able children need it?

It is arguable that all children benefit from enrichment of the curriculum but in the case of able children it is vital from the point of view of both the child and the school.

Many able children work very quickly and assimilate concepts rapidly. One of the most frustrating experiences for such children is to be forced to do repetitive exercises designed to help master a concept which they have already acquired. However from the teacher's point of view, this ability to acquire concepts can be a mixed blessing since a child who is excused practice exercises needs another activity to 'occupy' him or her for the given time. It would be ludicrous to suggest that enrichment activities are only made available on occasions such as these but if a child or group of children are involved in an ongoing enrichment activity, this may be a good time to pursue it.

Enrichment is also particularly good for able children because it can be interest-led. This can have a number of advantages. Firstly, it can allow able children to work at their own level with children of lesser ability approaching the same topic in a different way. This provides opportunities for meaningful mixed ability group learning and a chance for able children to pursue an activity to a level appropriate to them while at the same time remaining integrated in a group.

Secondly, it is possible to create a group of able children to work on an enrichment activity, thus allowing like minds to operate together within the classroom context, if other groups of children are involved with other enrichment activities from time to time. These 'created' team opportunities are particularly valuable for able children who tend to be isolated and have difficulties in forming relationships with other children.

Another advantage in interest-led enrichment is its inbuilt motivation. If a child is involved in an activity of her own choosing then not only will it probably use her ability to the full but it may also provide a useful situation in which the teacher can tackle aspects of the child's development which may be causing concern. For example, if a child is notoriously disorganised in her presentation of work, then a little judicious help with suitable ways to present information may be more easily accepted in the context of an interest-led enrichment activity than in a more formal setting of a core subject activity.

Finally, and perhaps most importantly, it can give the able child opportunities to plan her own work, evaluate her performance and pursue something she really enjoys to a level and in a way which suits her. Such opportunities are rare in general class activities and even the occasional chance will usually be greatly welcomed by the more able child.

Enrichment in the infant school

Many able children look forward to starting school because they see it as an opportunity to undertake all kinds of activities which have not been available to them at home. To begin with, school may well maintain this exciting image but all too often disillusionment quickly sets in. The children see that the majority of class time is spent developing basic skills which in some cases they have already acquired before beginning school. Little time is left for exploring those avenues which they might have found stimulating. Even in classes where much attention is given to meeting the needs of the individual, group activities like discussion are often at an inappropriate level. The more able the child, the further away he is from the majority of children in the class in terms of ability and interests. For these reasons enrichment is of key importance in the infant school.

Although these problems of performance may be at their most obvious in the infant age range, the infant environment also provides the most flexible and imaginative stage for enrichment activities. Most infant classrooms are full of displays, exhibits and information aimed at providing a stimulating environment. These can be used to maximum effect in appropriate enrichment activities. Able children can work with the materials that are in the classroom but use them in an imaginative way.

(a) QUESTIONS
One of the best ways to enrich an infant child's experience is by asking open-ended questions. Encourage children to speculate:

- Why do you think this happens?
- What would happen if?
- How could this be improved?

This can be applied to all aspects of the child's curriculum from prediction in books to hypothesis in science. Able children should learn not to look always for right answers but to seek possible solutions.

(b) OBSERVATION

In the same way, children should be encouraged to look carefully, to note differences and similarities and to observe how things happen. Close observation is an important habit for children to acquire and the infant environment provides myriad opportunities for this.

(c) STRUCTURE

Children should be encouraged to look at stages of development – in a butterfly, in a novel or in a piece of woodwork. They need to appreciate structure if they are to structure their own work.

It could be said that this type of enrichment would be useful to all young children and that may well be the case. It is, however, the kind of approach which able children can acquire quickly and then use with amazing effectiveness. Once they learn that knowledge is not gained exclusively either from adults giving out information or by them reading books, then they are able to make significant progress in some areas with minimum adult input. They do, of course, need opportunities to discuss their discoveries in a meaningful context, but children will in some ways generate their own work based on interests and previous discoveries.

Topic work in the infant school provides another good vehicle for enrichment. More challenging activities can be included, and since in most class topics all children do *not* do all the tasks, able children can be excused the simpler tasks in favour of one or two really challenging activities. A topic on colour, for example, could well lead more able children into science activities related to the light spectrum which might involve concepts too complex for most children of this age. Equally, in a topic on houses and homes, able children might be capable of looking in greater depth at the historical angle – comparing modern homes with those of previous generations. Children of all abilities might be able to tackle this to some degree but it has inbuilt opportunities for able children to pursue it further – and they will.

Enrichment should also be made available in the core subject areas. Many able young mathematicians acquire new numerical concepts very quickly and need minimal reinforcement. Their maths curriculum can be enriched by opportunities to explore early algebra in an interesting way, for example. They need to see maths as fun but it will not remain so if they have to plod through a maths scheme designed for children of lesser ability. In the same way maths investigations should be at a level appropriate to children's conceptual understanding. It is acceptable for an able child to tackle investigations which she finds easy

21

but sometimes she needs a real challenge. Similarly, in language it is fine to encourage able children to write their own books but sometimes it's more fun for them if you increase the challenge: 'Write a book for a child visiting England from another country' for example.

With infant children there is often a conflict between abilities and skills. Some children are able to read and write very quickly but many take as long if not longer than other children to *acquire* these skills. Imagine the frustration: a mind with a working vocabulary which many adults might envy and yet struggling to write three-letter words without reversals. This is not an easy problem to resolve. Such children have to acquire the skills while at the same time maintaining their lively and enquiring minds. It would be foolish to underestimate the difficulties involved here but their need for skills should not over-shadow their need for enrichment. Thinking power is just as important as recording skills. If these children are not given appropriate enrichment then by the time they have acquired written skills they will have little meaningful to convey.

Enrichment in the junior school

From the teacher's point of view enrichment experiences in the junior age range may prove easier to organise, particularly if the child has experienced enrichment in the infant years. He will already be accustomed to having a role in planning and evaluating work and this can be increased to an ever more sophisticated level as the child develops. By the time they reach the upper junior stage most children will greatly enjoy and be very skilled at negotiating tasks. They will have developed clear views about the subject areas they would like to tackle and the teacher's role may no longer be to encourage the child to explore beyond the areas undertaken by most children but to ensure that he covers the areas which are central to the topic and not just explore avenues which look interesting.

In much the same way junior pupils will be accustomed to observing closely and asking the 'Why?' questions. They will be adept at discovering problems which they wish to explore and, as it becomes increasingly tempting to spend large amounts of time on enrichment activities, the teacher may well need to be mindful that enrichment is not an alternative but an addition to mainstream approaches.

New enrichment approaches can be added in the junior school as the child acquires more skills. Once children can use a library, for example, then their access to information is greatly increased. Topic work in the

Figure 2.1: *Skills acquired through topic work*

Listening ← Talking ← Reading ← Writing
       →   →   →

Higher Order Reading Skills
- using a library
- using reference books (eg tables of contents and indexes)
- using encyclopedias.

Study Skills
- encouraging independent study requiring the ordering of work and time
- research (eg acquiring information from prime and secondary sources, artefacts, pictures, maps and diagrams)
- observation
- precise and divergent thinking
- using information and knowledge across the curriculum
- note-taking
- skimming and scanning.

Analysis and Evaluation
- understanding the facts
- questioning critically
- making references, speculating
- decision-making
- forming judgments and opinions
- appreciating accuracy, bias and propaganda
- communicating.

Synthesis
- using information
- rearranging material to develop new patterns and structures
- hypothesising
- proposing alternatives and improvements
- problem-solving.

Empathy
- developing sympathetic and understanding attitudes.

Skills specific to history and geography can also be included.

junior school is a good source of enrichment activities. Once again, able children can be presented with more challenging tasks within the context of a class topic. Many examples of this approach are now commercially available (see Chapter 9) and the ideas within them can be adapted to suit any topic and any learning environment.

The child's increased reading and writing skills will open up a wide range of information to him as he is able to read and work with adult materials. This is a great asset in terms of making tasks real and relevant. A child can handle the computer print-out of accident statistics (for example, Motorways LDA 1982, workstudy pack) and use them to make recommendations. He can extract information from the local papers and the public records office and use it to explore issues and form judgments. Some of the skills which able children might use in topic work are shown in Figure 2.1 above. These skills were drawn together by a group of colleagues working on enrichment materials. As well as being useful for the individual teacher, in staff meetings a skills sheet of this sort helps to focus discussion about enrichment.

Independent learning may allow a child at this stage to undertake a topic of his own which he can develop in a way appropriate to his skills and interests. This may or may not have any connection with topics being worked on by other members of the class. If, for example, the class were doing a topic on transport, able children could easily select one aspect of this subject and pursue it in some depth. Equally, they could have a personal topic based on their own interests which they undertake either in addition to or alongside the class topic or topics.

In the core areas, particularly maths and science, providing suitable enrichment materials may present some teachers with quite a challenge. It is not always easy to find related problems or harder problems in an area where you have limited expertise. The teacher may have to be more creative in finding ways to meet the challenge. Sometimes this can be done by having access to a wide variety of 'ideas books' on a particular subject – there are some very good maths books available for example (see Chapter 9 and Bibliography). Another approach is to find and make use of some specialist expertise in the area. This could be the school maths/science expert, a colleague from the secondary sector, maths/science support teams or an individual in the community.

It would be unrealistic to expect primary teachers to have in-depth knowledge of all areas of the curriculum, but able children are often given opportunities for enrichment only in those areas where the individual teacher feels academically comfortable, rather than in the areas which might be appropriate for the child. It is important to recognise that the need for outside input is not a failure on the part of the teacher – it is simply a recognition of the exceptional ability of the child.

Enrichment in the secondary school

Providing enrichment in the secondary school is subject to organisational constraints not apparent in the primary sector. Should enrichment be made available through the special needs department? Should it be available only on certain days of the year? Is it necessary in all subjects? How often should it occur? These are the type of questions which often emerge in secondary school discussions on enrichment. Such issues need to be addressed in conjunction with discussions on enrichment content since school timetables and general organisation are likely to have a significant influence on the type of enrichment made available.

(a) SPECIAL NEEDS ENRICHMENT
In some schools able children are seen as part of the special needs responsibility. They are identified as being in this category upon entry to school or, if appropriate, at a later date, and it then becomes the responsibility of the special needs department to ensure that appropriate provision is made for them. One way is for the special needs department to run enrichment sessions. These are usually once or twice a term and children are excused from ordinary lessons to attend. The object of running these sessions is to provide opportunities for children of similar ability to work together.

The enrichment session usually takes the form of an exploration of one interest or subject area. For example, a secondary school ran an enrichment day on the media. Students were asked to work in a newsroom and to produce a news bulletin at the end of the day. During the course of the day new stories were introduced constantly and for each one appropriate copy had to be written. Editors had to decide on the length and relative importance of stories and their mode of presentation with a view to producing a news broadcast of a given length. Shortly before transmission time a major new story broke and adjustments had to be made accordingly!

This kind of enrichment provides plenty of scope in an exciting format. Students needed to make use not only of academic skills but also of decision-making and negotiation skills. The group had to work effectively as a team and therefore some feeling of ownership for the project developed. The final aspect of the media project was a visit to a local radio station to discuss how news programmes are developed and so the dimension of using outside expertise was added. The students have since worked together at subsequent enrichment sessions including a weekend residential inquiry into geology.

(b) LEARNING SUPPORT

Some secondary schools now use their special needs department, either partly or totally, in a learning support role. This involves the special needs teacher supporting either the child or the teacher as appropriate. Therefore, a learning support teacher could take the majority of the class to free the class teacher to work with a group of more able children. Similarly, he or she could work within the classroom with a group of more able children developing further the work being undertaken by the class. This approach has the advantage of allowing children opportunities for enrichment without withdrawing or isolating them from other children.

(c) SUBJECT ENRICHMENT

This is, of course, central to the needs of the able child in the secondary school but is difficult to provide effectively, not least because of the number of personnel involved. Some schools have tackled the problem at departmental level with all members of a particular department working together to develop an approach. Here the elements of enrichment and extension are interwoven in that a department will need to decide not only what enrichment should entail but also the proportion of time which may appropriately be given to it.

It could be said that enrichment within subjects is mainly a part of effective curriculum differentiation. If a teacher is to make appropriate provision then any task or lesson should be seen in terms of how it could be simplified for the less able and made more challenging for the more able. In some cases this may mean the more able taking the concept further and in others addressing a related concept. For example, while others learn plane trigonometry the more able may tackle spherical trigonometry.

With exceptional children it may be necessary to develop this approach further and the more exceptional the child the more difficult it becomes. Teachers may need to consider the use of a 'mentor' for the student either from inside the school or an outside expert. This person would provide the student with intellectual stimulus and personal support. If the requirements of the National Curriculum are to be met then flexibility of organisation will undoubtedly increase. This should mean that the use of a mentor or other external influences should no longer single out a child as odd, strange or an intellectual phenomenon but simply be seen in the context of appropriate provision. As the numbers of children experiencing a non-standard timeable increase, for whatever reason, the idea of mentoring becomes more acceptable.

Organisation may again dictate enrichment. If a child's programme of work differs radically from that of her peers in a given subject, how will the programme be monitored etc? It should also be remembered that enrichment is not something which needs to be provided all the time.

(d) HOMEWORK ENRICHMENT

Some schools use homework as a way of providing enrichment for the more able. Students can be given thought-provoking tasks which may be cross-curricular. A good example of this is found in Barry Teare's Merlin Packs (see Chapter 9) – lots of ideas for short tasks which challenge and amuse. Also homework may provide a good forum for a subject enrichment task especially if the task makes use of outside resources and expertise. Local environmental issues, for example, could usefully be explored at least partially at home. Schools looking to meet the needs of the more able for the first time sometimes find homework a good way to introduce enrichment which can then be extended into a wider context.

(e) SUPPORTED SELF-STUDY, OPEN LEARNING, ETC

Many new approaches which may well contribute to enrichment for the more able are becoming available to schools. Some of these approaches have great flexibility and therefore are well suited to use with the more able. It is important to resist the temptation to put enrichment for able children in one category. Rather it should be that all new initiatives – information technology, TVEI, supported self-study, computers, etc – should be considered in terms of their enrichment potential. High ability in CDT needs appropriate enrichment just as much as high ability in more traditional areas.

(f) TRANSITION

One way in which secondary schools can facilitate easy transition from primary to secondary for the more able is to run enrichment sessions for their feeder primary schools. As well as having obvious benefits in terms of continuity, this allows primary schools access to secondary expertise and facilities and helps secondary colleagues to obtain a clearer view of the needs of more able individuals prior to their arrival in school. Like-minded children also have the chance to meet together and develop a positive attitude towards their new school which is particularly helpful in the case of sensitive children.

Models of enrichment

The idea of enriching the curriculum to meet the needs of the more able has been developed by some American psychologists to a sophisticated degree. The two exponents who have had the most significant impact on British thinking in this area are Benjamin Bloom and Joseph Renzulli.

Bloom, in his *Taxonomy of Educational Objectives* (1956), divided learning into six areas – knowledge, comprehension, application, analysis, synthesis and evaluation. The first three categories are commonly found in most children's education and account for a significant amount of time in the school day. The latter three are less common but in many ways require more complex thinking skills. In Figure 2.2 the school board in Wisconsin, USA has defined all six categories and given examples of how they may be incorporated into schooling.

In Britain, teachers in the field of education for the more able have found that incorporating opportunities for analysis, synthesis and evaluation into the curriculum has substantial benefits for the more able. Tasks involving these kinds of concepts are challenging because they require children to adopt more diverse approaches and strategies in their thinking. It is easy to see how classroom teachers can incorporate these concepts into their planning without any major adjustments to their established method of working. Obviously, this has attractions and so Bloom's taxonomy could, and in some schools does, form the basis of a school approach to the more able.

Joseph Renzulli has developed a triad model which he uses in developing programmes for the gifted (Renzulli, 1977). He sees programmes as needing three different types of activity if all aspects of a child's potential are to be developed (see Figure 2.3). As is evident in Figure 2.3 these types of activity are closely linked and children move between them freely. Renzulli sees type 1 and 2 tasks as being applicable to most children but it may be that only the more able will be able to tackle type 3. This then is very much in keeping with the British view that provision for the more able should, wherever possible, be an inclusive rather than an exclusive activity. In all three types of activity (see Figure 2.4) the emphasis is on the child's active involvement with him taking increasing responsibility for his own work.

Type 1 activities are already to be found in most of our schools in

Figure 2.2: *Bloom: definitions and examples*

	KNOWLEDGE	COMPREHENSION	APPLICATION	ANALYSIS	SYNTHESES	EVALUATION
DEFINITION	1. that which one knows; whether through study or experience. 2. the range of one's information or understanding.	1. understanding; the ability to understand.	1. putting something to use. 2. relate or apply ideas to new or unusual situations.	1. separation of a thing into its parts or elements to find out what it is made of. 2. careful examination.	1. to make or create new or original 'things'. 2. to think creatively.	1. make judgments about 'things'. 2. rate ideas, conditions, objects.
EXAMPLE	List our state/federal legislators. Identify the committee through which every piece of legislation must go.	Explain the need for gifted legislation to your legislator. Offer three ways your child would benefit if there were a programme to meet individual needs.	Use what you know (data) to find and offer solutions to the problem of state/ federal gifted monies being available to schools in your area.	Uncover the unique characteristics of various gifted and talented programmes currently receiving federal monies. Examine existing gifted and talented legislation to discover possibilities that already exist.	Create an advisory committee to support legislative efforts. Develop a piece of legislation which would benefit gifted and talented children.	Judge which items should be included in gifted and talented legislation. Decide which candidate would best represent gifted and talented efforts at a state and/or federal level.
EXAMPLE	Recite five characteristics of a gifted person. List five characteristics of a talented person.	Explain the six areas of gifted and talented proposed by the federal govt. Explain how to ask questions which allow children to think.	Practise asking your child questions which allow many different responses.	Examine several 'ideas to try with gifted and talented at home'. Extract the basic principles included in each item.	Develop a proposed plan which describes 'the best' environment for a talented and gifted child.	Rate the environments of your child: home, school, community.

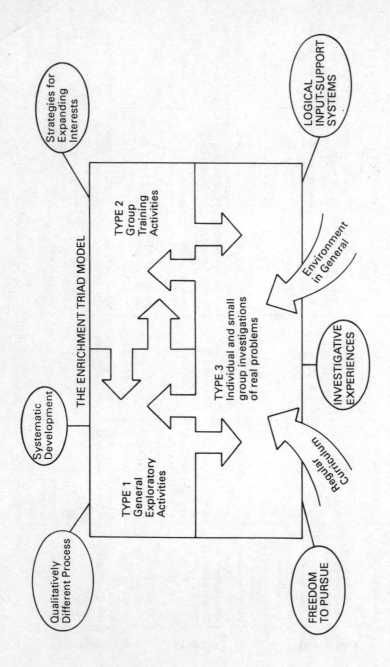

Figure 2.3: *The Renzulli Triad*

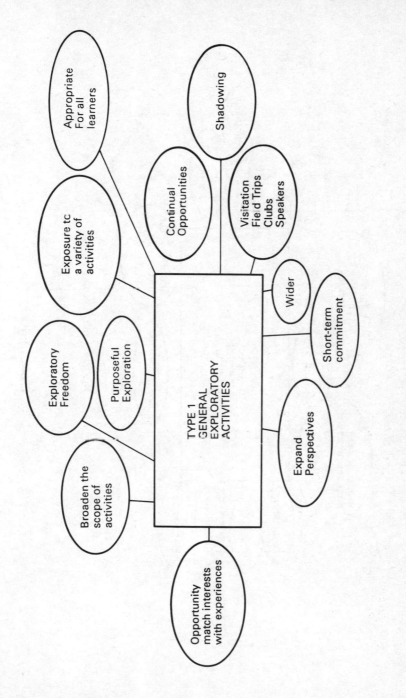

Figure 2.4: *Renzulli: a closer look at the model*

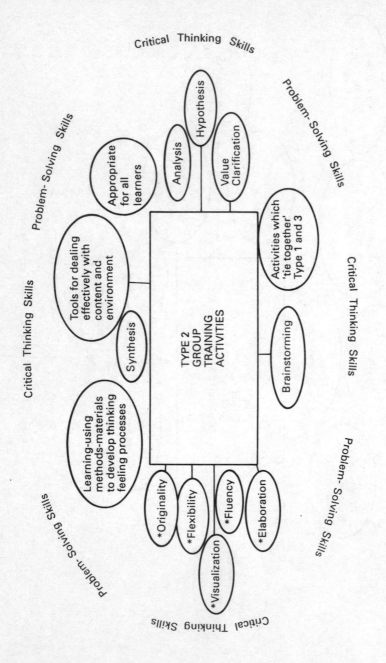

Figure 2.4: (cont)

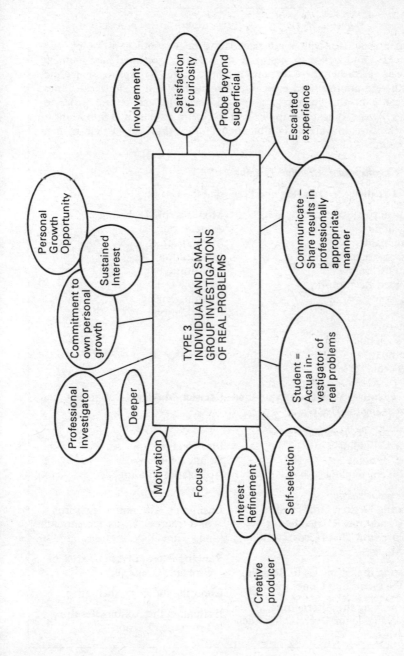

Figure 2.4: *(cont)*

Figure 2.5: *Taxonomy of type 2 enrichment processes*

Note: This taxonomy is not intended to be a complete listing of every thinking and feeling process, nor are the processes listed here mutually exclusive. Rather, there are many instances in which the processes interact with one another and even duplicate items from various categories. Because of this interaction, and the need to use several processes simultaneously in their application to real problems, it is important to teach them in various combinations rather than in an item-by-item fashion.

I. Cognitive and Affective Training

A. Creativity. Developing and Practising the Use of:

Fluency	Modification Techniques:
Flexibility	Adaptation
Originality	Magnification
Elaboration	Minification
Brainstorming	Substitution
Forced Relationships	Multiple Uses
Attribute Listing	Rearrangement
Fantasy	Combination
Imagery	Reversal
Association	
Comparison	
Risk-taking	

B. Creative Problem-Solving and Decision-Making: Developing and Practising the Use of:

Creative Problem-solving:

'Mess' Finding	Idea Finding
Fact Finding	Solution Finding
Problem Finding	Acceptance Finding

Decision-making:

Stating Desired Goals and Conditions Related to a Decision That Needs To Be Made	Examining Alternatives in Terms of Resources, Costs, Constraints and Time
Stating the Obstacles to Realising the Goals and Conditions	Ranking Alternatives in Terms of Probable Consequences
	Choosing the Best Alternative
Identifying the Alternatives Available for Overcoming Each Obstacle	Evaluating the Actions Resulting From the Decision

C. Critical Thinking. Developing and Practising the Use of:

Conditional Reasoning
Ambiguity
Fallacies
Emotive Words
Definition of Terms
Categorical Propositions
Classification
Validity Testing
Reliability Testing
Translation
Interpretation
Extrapolation
Patterning
Sequencing
Flow Charting
Computer Programming

Analogies
Inferences
Inductive Reasoning
Deductive Reasoning
Syllogisms
Probability
Dilemmas
Paradoxes

Analysis of:
Content
Elements
Trends and Patterns
Relationships
Organising Principles
Propaganda and Bias

D. Affective Training

Understanding Yourself
Understanding Others
Working with Groups
Peer Relationships
Parent Relationships
Values Clarification
Moral Reasoning
Sex Role Stereotypes
Assertiveness Training
Self Reliance
Dealing with Conflict

Coping Behaviours
Analysing Your Strengths
Planning Your Future
Interpersonal Communication
Developing Self-confidence
Developing a Sense of Humour
Showing an Understanding of
  Others
Dealing with Fear, Anxiety and
  Guilt
Dealing with the Unknown

II. Learning How to Learn Skills

A. Listening, Observing and Perceiving. Developing and Practising the Use of:

Following Directions
Noting Specific Details
Understanding Main Points, Themes and Sequences
Separating Relevant from Irrelevant Information
Paying Attention to Whole–Part Relationships
Scanning for the 'Big Picture'
Focusing in on Particulars
Asking for Clarification

Asking Appropriate Questions
Making Inferences
Noting Subtitles
Predicting Outcomes
Evaluating a Speaker's Point of View

B. Note-taking and Outlining. Developing and Practising the Use of:

Note-taking:
Selecting Key Terms, Concepts, and Ideas; Disregarding Unimportant
   Information
Noting What Needs to be Remembered
Recording Notes and Underlining or Highlighting the Most Important
   Items
Categorising Notes in a Logical Order
Organising Notes so that Information from Various Sources can be added
   at a Later Time

Outlining:
Using Outline Skills to write Material that has Unity and Coherence
Selecting and Using a System of Notation such as Roman Numerals
Deciding whether to Write Topic Outlines or Sentence Outlines
Stating Each Topic or Point Clearly
Using Parallel Structure
Remembering that each Section must have at least Two Parts

C. Interviewing and Surveying. Developing and Practising the Use of:

Identifying the Information Being Sought
Deciding on Appropriate Instrument(s)
Identifying Sources on Existing Instruments
Designing Instruments (eg Checklists, Rating Scales, Interview
   Schedules)
Developing Question Wording Skills (eg Factual, Attitudinal, Probing,
   Follow-Up)
Sequencing Questions
Identifying Representative Samples
Field Testing and Revising Instruments
Developing Rapport with Subjects
Preparing a Data Gathering Matrix and Schedule
Using Follow-Up Techniques

D. Analysing and Organising Data. Developing and Practising the Use of:

Identifying Types and Sources of Data
Identifying and Developing Data Gathering Instruments and Techniques

Developing Data Recording and Coding Techniques
Classifying and Tabulating Data
Preparing Descriptive (Statistical) Summaries of Data (eg Percentages, Means, Modes, etc)
Analysing Data with Inferential Statistics
Preparing Tables, Graphs and Diagrams
Drawing Conclusions and Making Generalisations
Writing Up and Reporting Results

III. Using Advanced Research and Reference Materials

A. Preparing for Type 3 Investigations

Developing Time Management Skills
Developing a Management Plan
Developing Problem Finding and Focusing Skills
Stating Hypotheses and Research Questions
Identifying Variables
Identifying Human and Material Resources
Selecting an Appropriate Formal and Reporting Vehicle
Obtaining Feedback and Making Revisions
Identifying Appropriate Outlets and Audiences

B. Library Skills

Understanding Library Organisational Systems
Using Information Retrieval Systems
Using Interlibrary Loan Procedures
Understanding the Specialised Types of Information in Reference Books
Such as:

Bibliographies	Periodicals	Yearbooks
Encyclopedias	Histories and	Manuals
Dictionaries and	Chronicles of	Reviews
Glossaries	Particular Field,	Readers' Guides
Annuals	Organisations	Abstracts
Handbooks	Concordances	Diaries
Directories and	Data Tables	Books of Quotations,
Registers	Digests	Proverbs, Maxims
Indexes	Surveys	and Familiar Phrases
Atlases	Almanacs	Source Books
	Anthologies	

Understanding the Specific Types of Information in Non-Book Reference Materials Such as:

Art Prints	Globes	Films
Talking Books	Maps	Study Print
Video Tapes/Discs	Film Loops	Models
Microforms	Pictures	Filmstrip with Sound
Filmstrips	Records	Flashcards
Transparencies	Slides	Audio Tapes
	Charts	Data Tapes

C. Community Resources

Identifying Community Resources Such as:
Private Businesses and Individuals
Governmental and Social Service Agencies
College and University Services and Persons
Clubs, Hobby and Special Interest Groups
Professional Societies and Associations
Senior Citizen Groups
Art and Theatre Groups
Service Clubs
Private Individuals
Museums, Galleries, Science Centres, Places of Special Interest or Function

IV. Developing Written, Oral and Visual Communication Techniques

A. Visual Communication. Developing Skills in the Preparation of:

Photographic Print Series
Slide Series
Filmstrips
Audio Tape Recordings
Overhead Transparencies
Motion Pictures
Video Tape Recordings
Multimedia Images

B. Oral Communication. Developing and Practising the Use of:

Organising Material for an Oral Presentation
Vocal Delivery
Appropriate Gestures, Eye Movement, Facial Expression and Body Movement
Acceptance of the Ideas and Feelings of Others
Appropriate Words, Quotations, Anecdotes, Personal Experiences, Illustrative Examples and Relevant Information
Appropriate Use of Audio Visual Materials and Equipment
Obtaining and Evaluating Feedback

C. Written Communication

Planning the Written Document (eg Subject, Audience, Purpose, Thesis,
Tone, Outline, Title)
Choosing Appropriate and Imaginative Words
Developing Paragraphs with Unity, Coherence and Emphasis
Developing 'Techniques' (eg Metaphor, Comparison, Hyperbole,
Personal Experience)
Writing Powerful Introductions and Conclusions
Practising the Four Basic Forms to a Variety of Games (ie Short Stories,
Book Reviews, Research Papers, etc)
Developing Technical Skills (eg Proofreading, Editing, Revising,
Footnoting, Preparing Bibliographies, Writing Summaries and
Abstracts)

Britain. Type 2 activities follow the Bloom pattern more closely and
can be seen in greater detail in Figure 2.5. These have been more
apparent in British schools over the last ten years or so but are still
comparatively underused, especially in primary schools. Type 3
activities refer to real problem-solving by individuals or small groups.
This type of activity has developed in maths in Britain especially in the
post-Cockcroft era but is not so widespread in other areas of the
curriculum.

The Renzulli approach, like Bloom's, was developed for the
American education system which has less emphasis on meeting the
needs of the individual. However, many of his ideas can be successfully
adapted for the British system and incorporated into general classroom
teaching. They provide a good framework for schools exploring the
needs of the more able and could provide the basis for a school
enrichment programme. Certainly, they are a useful focus for staff-
room discussion as colleagues may well have strong views on which
aspects of children's potential need more opportunities through
enrichment and whether this model is an effective response to those
needs. Traditionally, British schools have made little use of models as
methods of teaching (although many models have influenced our
practice informally), but in the case of enrichment it is useful to have a
concrete basis for discussion otherwise it could appear to be a concept
which is difficult to define and therefore difficult to convey to
colleagues.

Chapter 3
What is Extension?

If enrichment of the curriculum is taken to mean adding opportunities to those normally made available to children then extension is allowing children to move through the curriculum at a faster rate either by covering it more quickly or by skipping sections. Often the titles curriculum enrichment and extension are used interchangeably and it is easy to see how this occurs. If, for example, a child is being stretched and challenged in an enrichment activity then this too is a form of extension. In fact, much extension does take place in enrichment activities but to use the terms interchangeably draws attention away from the central issue of extension within the National Curriculum.

When and how much to extend a child is often a difficult decision for a school and an extreme stance may be adopted. One school may advocate a policy that all extension should come through enrichment and no child be allowed to move ahead in the 'normal' curriculum. Another school faced with the same child may well decide to move her up a class and assume that this will automatically meet the extension needs. Both these responses, while administratively attractive, fail to recognise the complexity of the extension needs of more able children. In the first case, an initial interest in the wide variety of activities available will soon give way to frustration if they did not present opportunities to work in depth. Equally, a child who is moved up a class may still operate at a level substantially above that of her new peers and so continue to encounter frustration. It would be unusual for either of these strategies to be successful in the long term and may well create rather than solve problems for the child.

Children do need opportunities to move ahead in the 'normal' curriculum. The problem is deciding when and how much. Extension can be harmful if it means the child is put under too much pressure but conversely the lazy child or the hesitant child may well need a judicious push. Good extension is for the most part child led. If a child is keen to move ahead then she should be allowed to do so. In fact, it is quite likely that the child will move ahead intellectually regardless of the artificial barriers which schools may create in the form of inappropriate tasks. However, these barriers are not only frustrating but also prevent the child from being exposed to real challenge and so hinder her progress. Schools and teachers seeking to help children fulfil their potential should encourage and support them to progress at a rate with which they feel comfortable and make appropriate provision within the school for this to be a realistic objective, however difficult that may be. For some children this will mean extension opportunities in all subjects but a far greater percentage may need extension opportunities in one or a limited range of subjects.

Even with the willing child it is important to monitor extension opportunities to ensure that they remain at an appropriate level. There may well be times when extension is not appropriate, when a child has a plateau in learning or a reflective period, for example. While in theory we know that these peaks and troughs in learning exist, in practice it is tempting to ignore them since a gradual progression would be so much more convenient. This could mean that what had begun as good child-led extension would become bad teacher-led extension.

The less overtly willing child is more of a problem. Hesitant children often need to move ahead but require a very secure environment in which to achieve this. Failure has to be seen as part of the learning process and not something which in some way diminishes the individual. Here extension may need to be gradual, an occasional taste to begin with and perhaps a more sustained dose later. With the lazy child sometimes the challenge sparks the interest and so solves the difficulty; if not, then the teacher, perhaps in consultation with head and parents, needs to decide how much pressure can be successfully applied. Usually, self-motivation is eventually reached with most able children but it would be a pity for a child to miss opportunities which would be enjoyable because of a lack of motivation.

Bad extension occurs when children are hustled either by school or by parents and this does not benefit the child but provides a vicarious gratification for the 'pusher'. For example, sometimes children may be academically ready to move ahead but not emotionally ready to cope with public exams. Education is not a race but a response to children's needs whatever they may be. Some able children may take exams early but it does not make them less able if they do not. Too much inappropriate pushing may lead to 'burn out' and disappointment for all concerned.

Extension is thus both a joy and a responsibility for schools. A joy in that a child or children may have the ability to make the most effective use of our education system but a considerable responsibility in deciding how this can best be achieved. The extension issues vary with age and environment but one factor remains constant: no child should be held back from her natural growth rate, so when a child wants to move on to a book or concept from the next National Curriculum attainment level, schools should respond positively.

How can appropriate extension be provided?

Long ago – before Plowden – able children found themselves, on entering school, forced to start from what the school deemed to be the beginning in reading, writing and number and to move through an established curriculum at a rate thought to be appropriate for children of that age. Today of course we are much more enlightened! None the less, elements of this philosophy still persist in some schools. This is usually not a result of an adherence to the philosophy of all children doing the same work at the same time but rather a response to professional concerns and anxieties.

For example, reading: while most teachers would agree that a child should progress at a speed appropriate to his ability in this area, some schools require children to start at the beginning of a reading scheme and read through the scheme until they hit the appropriate level. This is not because teachers wish to penalise good readers but because they lack the confidence to decide on what might be an appropriate level and so go for safety. Even in schools which use a real book approach to reading, infant classrooms seldom contain books which appeal to the child who habitually reads the family newspaper before setting out for school! Children who come to school as fluent readers are not so rare that provision for them does not need to be considered.

In the same way many teachers, even when aware of a child's aptitude for maths, insist that the child completes concrete experience tasks as a sort of insurance that the concepts have been properly acquired – the 'better to be safe than sorry' method. Unfortunately, while this may provide reassurance for the teacher it can generate disenchantment in the pupil. Therefore, the first aspect of extension must be starting children at the right level.

In addition, if a child is to be allowed to start at a level appropriate to his ability and then to progress rapidly, skipping some parts of the curriculum, the need for careful planning, monitoring and professional decision-making is greatly increased. Hence the problem: how can this

be done in large mixed ability classes? And even if it can, is it desirable for a child to move far ahead of his peers and risk social isolation? There are no precise answers to these questions but they do warrant closer consideration.

Allowing or encouraging children to move ahead at their own rate has, in theory, been possible in primary schools for some time but in practice it is usually only possible in subject areas where the school adheres to a set scheme and consists of moving further through the scheme. In fact, it may be that with the advent of the National Curriculum teachers will find it easier to cater for children who need to move ahead in a wide variety of subject areas in that the contents of the next stage of progression are determined in National Curriculum documents. This does not dispense with the organisational problems but it does help with the 'what should be taught next?' aspect. Also, when planning is done with National Curriculum attainment targets in mind, teachers will be making provision for children to experience elements of levels above that expected of their age range to allow for the needs of the more able, as part of the differentiated curriculum. So limited extension opportunities will (or should be) inbuilt.

If children are capable of working at levels significantly above their age-expected level then this may well create large organisational problems in that the required resources and/or the teacher expertise may not be available. It would be possible to address this problem by allowing more fluidity between year groups – children working with older pupils in some subjects, for example – but this creates significant problems in timetabling in large schools and can have implications for the social integration of some more able children.

The whole question of to what extent children should be extended and enriched is discussed in more detail in Chapter 4, but for most able children some extension is both necessary and desirable if they are to be challenged and fulfilled. This is bound to set them apart from their peers to some extent and so it is important that schools create a climate where it is acceptable to move ahead. From conversations with able children, it sometimes appears that in trying to reduce the feelings of failure for less able children in school, we have created an environment where able children feel guilty about their ability and do not like to display it.

'Always in England if you had the type of brain that was capable of understanding TS Eliot's poetry or Kant's logic, you could be sure of finding large numbers of people who would hate you violently.' (DJ Taylor)

Education is, of course, about allowing *all* children to maximise their

potential, whatever that may be, and therefore able children must have the opportunities and encouragement to move ahead if appropriate.

Starting school

As has been mentioned previously some children may come to school with abilities and skills considerably above those expected for their age range, and it is important that appropriate provision is made for them immediately. Here parents can play an important role. In an era where education is in the public domain and seldom a week passes without some educational comment in the media, many parents have acquired the skill to look at their children in the same way as schools. They know if their child can recognise her letters, add up, etc, not to mention where she might come on the National Curriculum levels, and the parents of many able children can give the school the first clues about a child's potential.

Indeed many parents may also have strong views on how they would like the school to respond to their child's abilities and the potential for conflict is considerable. Hence, not only are parents very useful in giving the school a clear view of their child but also the school may help the parents to understand the importance of blending enrichment and extension opportunities in their child's academic progress. Traditionally, parents of able children hope to see them progress rapidly through school and strongly resist any 'holding back'. Schools need to explain in terms which parents can understand the need for enrichment and also the importance of social integration.

Able children need happiness and fulfilment as well as academic success and most parents of able children are anxious for their children to achieve all three. Since the provision made for an able child in terms of both enrichment and extension may well differ from that made available to other children it is important that home and school work together. Many parents are very supportive if they feel that the school is taking the trouble to meet their child's needs but confusion and mistrust occur when a school takes what it considers to be appropriate action without discussing this with the parents.

For example, a school bases much of its maths work around a scheme, but decides that it would be more appropriate for Peter to spend less time on the commercial scheme, which he manages with ease, and more time on a range of other extension activities which would provide more real challenge. The parents' expectation is that Peter will simply work his way through the scheme faster than other children and may well be surprised and disconcerted to learn that this

does not occur in the way they had envisaged. Of course, if the school talks to the parents about their plans for Peter's mathematical progress they will be reassured but otherwise, while the school feels it is making an appropriate response, the parents are fermenting unease and distrust which could easily have been avoided.

For many parents having a child of high ability is a heavy responsibility. School should be seen to provide the expertise to nurture that ability and be an ally in the desire to help that child fulfil his potential.

Extension in the infant school

It has sometimes been suggested that with young children it may be better to concentrate on enrichment and ignore extension altogether. This argument has several apparent flaws as any parent of an able child will tell you. It is impossible to stop children moving ahead in subjects which are of interest to them and to attempt to do so leads to frustration. This happens more than might be expected because some teachers feel that a stimulating, enriching classroom provides the able child with sufficient challenge without introducing advancement, particularly in core subjects. In some cases, so much emphasis is put upon the interest and stimulating nature of a task that its degree of difficulty is virtually ignored. Obviously the elements of enrichment and extension should work in harmony.

While a heavy emphasis can and should be placed on enrichment the infant child still needs tasks which respond appropriately to her abilities and skills. Often low expectation can lead infant teachers to be unaware of the capabilities of their more able children and so little extension material is made available.

Neville Bennett in *The Quality of Pupils' Learning Experiences* (1984) found that high attainers were underestimated on 40 per cent of the tasks assigned to them, and this is consistent with the findings of HMI surveys and other educational research.

If a child is asked to count the eight cars, colour them in and write the number, then that is what she will do – even if she can count to a hundred, a thousand or more.

In designing tasks for more able infants the teacher needs to be quite clear as to the objective. Many children may operate in National Curriculum level 3 in speaking and listening but only level 1 in writing and spelling. Therefore, if a task incorporates a combination of skills, a mismatch may occur. Certainly, it would be immensely demoralising for a child to be given only level 1 experiences in speaking and listening activities simply because reading and writing skills were less developed than oral. In much the same way a child with a facility for numbers may exhibit less skill in spatial awareness tasks and the teacher needs to set other tasks accordingly.

Generally, much of the discussion regarding extension in infant schools focuses on the need to meet able children's intellectual needs while at the same time ensuring that they master those skills which will be essential if they are to progress effectively. Learning to write and spell is for most children a chore no matter how imaginatively it is presented, yet these skills are essential tools which must be acquired. In extending the curriculum for able infants it is important not to stunt a child's intellectual development by insisting that all activities require the use of these basic skills.

A child's ability to argue a case, or relate events in sequence is not related to the ability to draw letters or spell words. One 6-year-old of my acquaintance is well able to explain the effect of chlorofluorocarbons on the ozone layer, including the basic chemistry, but is unable to read fluently or to write legibly. However, a neglect of the emphasis on basics can mean that an able child is hindered in her later progress by being unable to read or write at an appropriate level. The answer to all this has to lie in careful teacher planning and monitoring progress. The more the child deviates from the expected norms the more crucial this becomes. High teacher expectation is essential but so too is the sensitivity to recognise the child's limits at any given time.

All infant children should be encouraged to seize opportunities and to move ahead as quickly as they are able. Bright infant children should not be given ceilings (the 'we don't cover that until the juniors' attitude) but encouraged to tackle any problems which they wish to pursue and be congratulated on their achievements. This academic success should be recognised and applauded in the same way as we might applaud a talented musician or sportsperson, not because their ability makes them better than other children but because perseverance has led to outstanding achievement.

As teachers we must learn to have confidence in the assessments we make of young children and to act upon those assessments. Few teachers, when asked to nominate the more able children in their class, are prepared to name them unless the child is truly outstanding in every way. At infant level this happens with less able children too. The feeling is that it is too early to tell. In the case of more able children (and perhaps less able too!) it doesn't really matter that we are uncertain of the degree of potential. The child is not being placed in an artificial category for life – it is simply a rule of thumb to enable us to decide .

which children might need extension at a particular time. The amount of extension may well differ from child to child and it can be that six months later the group of children has altered with new potential being discovered and other children experiencing temporary plateaux. However, unless the teacher is actively seeking opportunities to extend, only those children whose ability is so exceptional that the teacher is unable to ignore it will benefit.

PROFILING EARLY ACHIEVEMENT
Of course this type of approach emphasises the need for good profiling systems. If children are to be allowed to move ahead then subsequent teachers need to be aware of the degree of advancement and its nature. Equally, it is important to document information on the child's weaknesses lest it be assumed that an ability in certain areas means an ability in all areas. All this may seem like a large amount of additional work for the teacher but it should be remembered that many underachievers and disruptive pupils are in fact of high ability and so channelling potential effectively can alleviate problems in other areas of classroom management.

Extension in the junior school

In most junior schools classroom management allows for a certain degree of advancement. While children are not formally setted they are usually grouped for at least some activities and these groups are often ability based. Hence the 'red group' in maths is effectively the top group since it works on the next stage in the scheme. For some able children this degree of extension may well be sufficient but problems can occur for a child who needs to move ahead faster than the rest of 'red group' or for a child whose investigative abilities are stronger than his numerical abilities. While he is in 'green group' for the maths-scheme-based work he may need to work with 'red group' or even beyond it in investigative tasks. One of the potential dangers in grouping is if it becomes too rigid.

However, some ability grouping can and does have advantages. It allows able children to move ahead together, so reducing feelings of social isolation, and ensures at least some inbuilt extension. It provides an opportunity for like minds to toss ideas about and so advance more rapidly. This is, of course, assuming that the groups are allowed to discuss and work together and the word group is not merely an administrative term meaning to set the same piece of work to be done in isolation.

Much of junior class work is not differentiated. In science, for example, all children may be set the same task or will undertake a series of tasks in rotation. Able children are not usually expected to draw more sophisticated conclusions or to offer more imaginative hypotheses. Here is an area where extension is in its infancy in many junior schools. With its heavy emphasis on science the National Curriculum will lead to children doing more science but as teachers we must also look to the extension opportunities which are available. If we do not expose children to ideas and concepts beyond those expected for their age range then it will be impossible for them to achieve higher levels of attainment. If, for example, in attainment target 1, Exploration of science, we do not introduce the concept of recording information in tables (level 4) to our bright 8-year-olds then they will not be aware of it as a possibility. This means we must always be alert for opportunities to introduce more advanced concepts to those who can handle them and so extension becomes an integral part of all classroom planning. This need not be restricted to those subjects covered by the National Curriculum but may also occur in, for example, drama and home economics.

Children do not necessarily need to be set different tasks or given different opportunities but can be extended within the same task. Adult conversation is very important here. The teacher needs to know which individuals are capable of a broader understanding of the task and should gauge questions appropriately. High expectation is essential and able children should come to understand that they will be expected to look beyond the obvious and to make critical responses. This kind of expectation tends to raise the performance level of most children in the class but able children can use it to maximum effect. Often, if an outside expert visits a school and the talk is pitched at a level rather above that which might be expected, children, in their desire to participate fully in the experience, manage to 'keep up'. The outcome is an understanding beyond that which might have been reasonably expected.

This indicates that we should not be afraid to experiment with pitching work or experiences at a higher level and evaluating their degree of success. Children can be extended, at least sometimes, more than we expect, especially if the subject is interesting and the approach lively.

The extension appropriate to some children may be substantially more advanced than the work customarily made available in a given class. This means that a teacher may need to look for outside help in both resources and expertise. Providing width and depth in enrichment can be daunting enough but to encounter a child or children in your class with a conceptual understanding of a subject which is beyond your own can be a very threatening experience. If appropriate extension is to be provided then the school needs to have accepted ways of supporting teachers in this provision. This may take the form of a teacher with expertise in a particular subject assisting another teacher in practical curriculum extension planning in respect of an individual or group of more able children. Equally, it may involve whole school planning or secondary school liaison or assistance from the LEA in terms of access to materials and expertise. Whatever strategies are used, this is not an area which can coexist with rigid attitudes. Very able children can be highly individualistic and extension opportunities must reflect this. They can also make teachers feel very inferior and so it is essential that teachers have adequate support otherwise there is a temptation to deny the need for extension through fear of being unable to provide it.

As able children reach the top of the junior school it is particularly essential that secondary colleagues are made aware of the extension work being provided. Firstly, it would be absurd for a child to have moved ahead substantially in the junior school and for this to be ignored in the secondary school. Secondly, close contact between the schools may allow appropriate responses to the child's needs to emerge to give good continuity across phase (see Patricia Marshall, *Transition and Continuity in the Educational Process* in this series). This may mean a teacher or teachers from the secondary school helping to plan the child's final-year primary work thus making it possible to continue in a similar vein when the child changes school, or it may involve the child visiting the secondary school for some lessons. Whatever strategy is adopted it is essential that it is evolved by both schools as equal partners otherwise the child or children can become unwilling pawns in a professional disagreement. The secondary school may feel that the primary has provided inappropriate extension opportunites which are impossible to maintain and the primary may feel that their secondary colleagues are not building on the good start which the child has experienced.

In short, able junior children should be allowed to continue the extension begun in the infant school. By the end of the junior school the gap (often called the 'four-year gap') between their achievements and those of their peers may well be considerable, particularly in individual subject areas. This means that the school may need to look outside to provide appropriate help and will almost certainly require close liaison with secondary schools to provide appropriate cross-phase continuity.

Extension in the secondary school

In most secondary schools it is possible to draw a clear distinction between extension made available for exceptional children and extension for the more able in general. Exceptional children are normally the subject of discussion even before they arrive at the school. There may well have been talk of sending the child a year early or the child may arrive with a cohort of children of a higher chronological age. In either case parents will have been involved as well as the child's primary or junior school. It is likely, whatever label is used by the school, that this child will be viewed as having special needs in the broadest sense of the term. Responsibility for her progress will be allocated to a specific member of staff be it within the special needs department, first-year tutors or senior management of the school. Discussion will take place regarding appropriate responses and the child's progress will be carefully monitored. However, it is largely dependent upon the school as to exactly how much the provision for this child will deviate from the norm.

In some schools a child of this type is simply seen as exceptional, especially if the high ability is in only one subject area, eg maths. The child is encouraged to join older groups of children for some or all maths lessons, may spend some individual time with maths teachers and, as she grows older, may have an out-of-school mentor from the local university perhaps. She could have access to the university facilities and no doubt that university would hope to see her as a student in the future. This type of approach is not unknown in the state system and has proved very successful for some children. It seems to happen most often in maths, and sometimes other sciences, because these are the subjects where children with exceptional conceptual understanding can move ahead most rapidly.

An approach of this kind is not without problems and some schools would consider it inappropriate. The child is without doubt seen as different although this does not necessarily lead to social isolation if the school is able to establish and maintain an appropriate climate. It is very difficult to timetable appropriate opportunities and it may well be that although a child would benefit intellectually from doing all maths lessons with an older age group a compromise is reached because of the administrative difficulties. The school may of course feel, with some justification, that it is to the child's benefit to spend some time with her own age range and so reduce the contact time with older children.

The crucial factor in all individual, exceptional cases is that the needs of the child should not be sacrificed to that great dictator of secondary schools – the timetable. The degree and nature of the extension for these children depend on the child, the school and the parents. Some children are not emotionally equipped to deal with excessive isolation from their peers; others are largely unconcerned. Some parents will see a route of this type as perfectly acceptable; others will consider it anathema. Some schools will be prepared to go to enormous lengths to uncover suitable opportunities and mentors; others will not.

Many parents of very able children feel that the state system is unable or unwilling to provide for them. Evidence does not indicate that this is true, but if parents are seeking an individually tailored response for their child they would be well advised to spend time choosing an appropriate state school. Some heads and schools feel that they cannot justify spending the amount of time required on one child. It is unlikely that an individual parent would be able to alter this view, but schools who adopt this stance should consider whether they would be prepared to devote equal time to a child with learning difficulties.

So a school meeting the needs of an exceptional individual may well have to tailor-make a programme of work but this will be easier if the school already has extension opportunities for its more able children. These are a far larger group and are likely to be the school's most successful pupils in academic terms. Provided that they reach their potential, they should be the public exam successes and later become successful in higher education. Because they are a far larger group, the school needs to consider their extension opportunities as part of a whole-school policy for more able children. This should include extension activities within the classroom and beyond it.

Firstly, the question of extension *within* the classroom. All subject departments need to decide what are appropriate extension opportunities within their subject and who might benefit from them. Denton and Postlethwaite (1985) refer to the need to identify children in subject specific terms. To this end they have compiled checklists in physics, French, maths and English. These lists have certain common elements but also have abilities relevant to that particular subject. They are an excellent focus for discussion among colleagues within that subject and also point towards the form which extension opportunities may take.

Within the National Curriculum the need to offer a differentiated approach is stressed. According to the guidelines a 13-year-old child might reasonably be expected to be achieving at between levels 3 and 8. This is an enormous difference. Staff will need to discuss how it might be possible to teach a lesson taking account of those widely differing needs. Fortunately, many standard lessons can be adapted, but as far as the more able are concerned discussion should focus not only on how this can be achieved but also the interpretation of some of the higher levels. Never before has there been such a national focus on extension within the classroom and a focus of this type may not only address, but also suggest, possible solutions for some of the issues involved.

Extension *beyond* the classroom is equally difficult to provide. The question of how much, and when, involves some of the issues relevant to younger children, and has the additional problems related to large schools and complex timetables. Large schools should mean greater opportunities and increased flexibility but this is sometimes difficult to achieve. The first stage is for staff to recognise that there might be a need to provide extension opportunities in some or all subjects for those who are able to take advantage of them. Some schools provide extension for school year groups; some target particular subjects. It is desirable but probably impractical to hope for more than this in the present climate of undermanning and competing needs, but priorities need to be decided by design rather than default.

Some schools use their learning support departments to free staff to teach extension groups and this is certainly a broader response to learning support provision. It is also a recognition that able children do have special needs and that the old idea that the top set should always be the biggest because those are the children who need least help is probably one of the major causes of underachievement among bright children.

Therefore, extension in the secondary school should be part of a considered response to the needs of the more able in the school. It should operate both inside and outside the classroom and in harmony with enrichment opportunities. Sometimes a child will have extension needs which are so far beyond her contemporaries that it is impossible to provide effectively within a group and in these cases an individual programme may need to be established. Adolescents who are not given opportunities for appropriate extension often discover other, less productive ways to spend their time. Then the school is forced to turn its attention to these children, but nothing useful has been achieved.

Acceleration

The question of whether it is appropriate to move a child up to the next class or to skip a complete year arises when a child has ability across a wide range of areas. At first glance it seems logical that if a child can operate at an academic level equivalent to the class above then that would be an appropriate place for him to be. There are, however, more complex and subtle issues which need to be considered before this kind of radical step is taken.

Firstly, there is the recognition that this step is essentially irreversible. If a child's development slows at a later stage it is not possible to put him back a class without causing feelings of acute failure. While we know that children do not progress on a steady course, making this decision based on academic needs implies that this progress will be maintained.

Secondly, a move of this kind has significant social implications. Children may well find it difficult to make friendships in this situation because even if a child is normally drawn towards playing with older children his new classmates may not necessarily treat him as an equal partner but rather as something strange and different and often unfortunately the subject of ridicule. Sometimes with young children this is not felt to be a problem especially in vertically grouped classes but it is important to remember that things may change as a child grows older. An immature 12-year-old girl may not have the same physical appearance as her more mature 13-year-old peers. A slight boy of the same age may find it additionally difficult to compete on the rugby or football field.

Thirdly, it should be acknowledged that moving a child forward a class may not provide appropriate extension opportunities. It may well be that the child's ability is such that he operates on a level above his new class and so extension may still need to be provided.

Finally, academic and emotional development are not always closely linked. A very bright child may be socially immature and totally unable to cope with the additional burdens of being in an exceptional environment.

Therefore, acceleration needs to be carefully considered. There are children for whom acceleration is entirely appropriate and very successful but they are not as numerous as might first appear. Acceleration should be a considered response to a child's needs not an easy way out of an administrative headache. It is more likely that a child may need to be accelerated in one or more subjects. This can allow a child to work at an appropriate level while still maintaining links with his age group. The risk of isolation is still present but not as pronounced, and in some cases is outweighed by the advantages of working with other children at the same academic level.

In some schools where children move groups and classes quite frequently it is possible for a child to spend time with older children without it appearing unnatural. The more this happens the more accepted it becomes. Ideally, it would be good if opportunities were available for children with abilities in different subjects to spend at least some time with older children so that X, Y and Z may join the class above for maths twice a week while P, Q and Y join them for language. Often this type of approach is rejected because it is assumed that if age barriers were made less important then the less able would have to work with younger children but there is no reason why this should have to occur.

No doubt secondary school teachers with responsibility for timetabling will be shaking their heads in horror, and with some justification, but it may be the case that it is only by providing more flexibility that it is possible to provide for the wide variety of levels of achievement which the National Curriculum will bring.

Conclusions

Extension opportunities need to be made available for all children who can take advantage of them, regardless of age. They need to be available in the classroom, beyond the classroom and, where relevant, beyond the school. Children should be encouraged to achieve and be rewarded for it, as a fulfilment of their potential. Failure to provide leads to disruptive children and major underachievement. Schools need to work with parents and other interested agencies in making available suitable opportunities and children should be encouraged but not pushed to take advantage of them.

In short, enrichment and extension should work together to provide a co-ordinated response to able children.

Chapter 4

The Two-way Stretch

In Chapter 2 we looked at enrichment. This we saw as a process of learning which involves staying with a theme, subject or topic or even a skill and working on it in *depth*.

Mainly enrichment

The following classroom activities are examples of learning which involve enrichment rather than extension:

1. A project on transport by a 13-year-old boy which involved mapping the whole of the London underground system including not only existing stations and tunnels but also all the disused tunnels and stations now shut down, in such a way as to reveal how the network has developed over the years.

2. A project which started from a group of children questioning why they could see rainbow patterns and colours in puddles. This led to a study of the spectrum, of how prisms 'break up' white light, refraction of light in water and glass, refractive indices, density, oil-films, and even the thickness of the thinnest oil-film possible – one molecule! From there it led on to weather studies, cloud formation, atmospheric pressure, wind formation, prevailing winds, plant distribution, fungi, bird migrations and conditions for growth and propagation.

3. Following a mathematics lesson a secondary class set out to find as many possible situations in real life that could be described or modelled by the equation $v = u + ft$. Suggestions included:

   - a car speed u and acceleration f has speed v after time t
   - a bank account £u with weekly saving £f amounts to £v after t weeks

- a poker length u cm, expanding f cm per °C, becomes v cm long after heating through t °C
- a spring u cm long, which stretches f cm per kg of load, becomes v cm long when a load t kg is added
- a phone bill £v was made up of the standing charge £u plus the cost of t calls at £f per call

and many others. The exercise resulted in a much clearer appreciation of the idea of a *linear* relationship than a straightforward drill exercise on the equation and led on to a lot of straight-line graph work involving the ideas of intercept, gradient, scale and intersection.

This and other examples of equations or functional relationships such as $pv = c$, $y = sin\ x$, each of which provides a mathematical model for a whole variety of practically different but essentially similar real situations, followed.

4. An English class took the theme 'Autumn' and searched out examples of its treatment in literature starting with Keats' 'Ode to Autumn' and moving on to other poems and prose passages. This led on to the 'autumn of life' generally – Shakespeare's 'Seven Ages of Man' and similar reflections. It might of course have been developed in biological terms – the 'fall', the process of ageing, the cycles of nature, and so on.

5. Another example of enrichment arose in a history lesson in a Nottingham school. The teacher was talking about the story of Robin Hood and the Sheriff of Nottingham and was telling the children that this was a legend, that Robin Hood probably never really existed. One little girl asked whether the story of Julius Caesar which they had done recently was also a legend. This, to the teacher's credit, led to a splendid discussion and some very valuable follow-up lessons on elementary ideas of historical evidence. It could take the form of handed down oral accounts, written accounts, official records, actual possessions, tangible works, and in recent times, paintings, photographs and recordings of the person in question. The class soon saw that some of these examples of evidence might be 'harder' or more convincing than other examples and that cases of genuine doubt could arise.

Later, this could have been pursued into the need for proof, the reason for legal trials, the debates about the authorship of Shakespeare's plays, the Turin Shroud, the existence of God, and so on. (Such a development would be more in the nature of an *extension* than a simple case of *enrichment*.)

6. Enrichment in sporting terms may involve many things. Within a school it may take the form of a wide and varied range of sports and games to pursue. In a boys' school visited recently it was possible to take part in football, athletics, cricket, hockey, swimming, volley-ball, judo, archery, golf, squash, badminton, fives and rowing. Within a single lesson a youngster may, at the cricket nets say, work on his run up, delivery, speed, spin, etc. On the tennis court basic stroke play can be developed through forehand, backhand and then volleying on both hands.

In one interesting lesson, the PE teacher had been discussing the question of balance and the things we can and cannot do with our bodies. This provoked a good discussion on the hazards of lifting heavy weights, swimming out of one's depth, over-exertion, strenuous movement before the muscles are warmed up, and so on to the kinds of injuries that might be sustained. In the activity which followed the pupils were told to work out and adopt a safe position of equilibrium using any of the apparatus in the gymnasium. A good variety emerged but in most cases the pupils were either standing, balancing or sitting *upright*. The teacher then asked them to discover different positions of balance in which their feet were *above* their heads.

7. Art offers many opportunities for enrichment (and extension). In almost any area of artistic activity enrichment is possible. In one water colour class, the students had mastered plain and graded washes and were freely experimenting with all kinds of other techniques to gain various effects. Some were practising wet-in-wet techniques at various stages of drying; others were sprinkling salt on drying washes to get snowstorm and 'rock texture' results; some were using toothbrushes to spray on over colour; one was investigating masking techniques of various kinds under washes.

8. Likewise in music, a taught skill can be enriched and given life beyond sterile repetition. In a small violin class students were playing the scale and arpeggio of C in first, third, fifth fixed positions and then moving positions on one or two strings to judge the final possibilities. In another group the partially mastered skill of vibrato was being practised at various speeds and then as wrist- and arm-originated vibrato. Vibrato in singing and string playing can add greatly to the richness of sound produced but if it is not varied in speed and breadth, and is used all the time, it can grow wearisome.

So enrichment may involve perfectionism, active complication of a skill or theme, rigour and substantiality.

Mainly extension

In Chapter 3 we looked at *extension* and saw this as a process of forging ahead, moving on to a higher skill or a more difficult concept.
  Commonplace examples of extension abound, including:

- going on to the next mathematics textbook
- studying the later, more difficult work of a poet
- moving on to the next tense, the next conjugation, the next construction in French or Latin
- going on to organic chemistry after inorganic chemistry
- using a more difficult medium in art – acrylics, oils, lino cut, perspex, polystyrene
- going on to diatonic music from the pentatonic, to atonal from tonal, serialism, minimalism etc
- going on to a more rigorous reapproach to the ideas of the calculus through analysis
- pursuing hierarchies of evidential argument in history.

All this is about progress and linear progression. In practice, the youngster who just cannot be held back, who makes inexorable progress, may need to skip a grade or even change schools. At the very least she will need to work with pupils of equal ability from time to time. It was for this reason that the Royal Institution mathematics master classes were set up whereby able young mathematicians could meet together each Saturday morning to do some really challenging mathematics together and take away some taxing work and problems for the rest of the week. Some schools welcomed this and reinforced encouragement and support at the school end. Sadly, other schools took no interest in this attempt to help those able mathematicians that they themselves had neglected.

Enrichment and extension

It is not easy to separate these two aspects of curriculum differentiation. Some of the examples quoted above undeniably include elements of both. Indeed, lots of school activities do. We can all think of the science project which cannot proceed without the learning of a new technique, or of the piece of music which cannot be played without mastering a new skill, or the piece of poetry whose references are unfamiliar and need to be read up.

Historically, there are many precedents for this. Scientific discovery has spawned a need for many new techniques. On the other hand, historical research has unearthed many new facts.

Thus, *many* activities involve both enrichment and extension. Most able pupils pursue both activities at one time or another or separately.

Simplistically, enrichment looks like this:

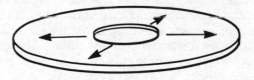

Extension looks like the forced stick of rhubarb:

Together enriched *and* extended growth looks like this:

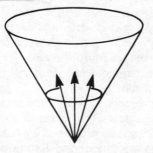

Most children, *overall*, grow like this, but in *particular* they don't quite grow like this *all the time*. The Plowden research and subsequent work of Professor JM Tanner, former Professor of Child Health and Growth, University of London, provided clear research evidence for the Plowden Committee that boys develop quite differently from girls. For both there are periods of rapid growth, stagnation, even fall back.

Strategies and ideas

1. SETTING
The oldest strategy for dealing with the ablest pupils and those most in need of curricular enrichment and extension is that of *setting*. In this, the ablest in each subject are grouped by ability. This enables the teacher to focus upon a relatively narrow band of ability. However, it must be remembered that a *truly gifted* child might be as far removed from his contemporaries in a top set as he would be in a mixed ability group.

2. GROUP WORK
Where it is possible to organise pupils in groups by interest or ability it is possible to cater for the ablest without undue difficulty. This strategy implies a range of material and the organisational freedom to treat each group differently.

3. INDIVIDUAL WORK
Individual work and tuition are very important. Sometimes, a bright child, far ahead of other children in the class, is simply the only one working on a particular project, task or book. Indeed, able youngsters often like to get on by themselves.

Many teachers believe that individual work is good for all children as it offers an opportunity for responsible self study. Schemes such as SMILE, the Kent Mathematics Project and the Heinemann Scottish Mathematics Scheme are each designed for individual learning. As a pupil finishes one piece of work she checks her answers, makes corrections and then moves on to the next. At the end of each unit or topic there is a self-assessment test before moving on to the next theme or topic in the overall scheme.

There are similar schemes in other subjects though they are usually topic-based and less sequential. In Chapter 9 we list a number of such individual learning materials produced by NACE (National Association for Curriculum Enrichment and Extension), Pullen Publications and by various LEAs.

4. INTEGRATED WORK

Most of the work in a good nursery or infant school is integrated. Children learn quite indiscriminately about numbers, measures, shapes, colours, materials, plants and animals, using their rapidly developing vocabularies and linguistic powers. They are not concerned with nice distinctions between historical, geographical and scientific aspects of things. But primary education is basically about discrimination and classification, so the subject divisions slowly acquire importance.

By the secondary school these subject divisions are clear and pronounced. The school day is usually fragmented by time and subject content. Indeed, the divisions can become overplayed and counterproductive. It is not uncommon to find that co-ordinates in mathematics are seen as quite different from grid references in geography simply because they arise in different subject lessons.

The links between subjects should not be lost and for many children should be constantly emphasised. However, the ablest will use such connections unbidden. Just as for Leonardo da Vinci knowledge, science and art seemed to be all one, so integrated work may help able pupils to see the wood for the trees more clearly. In a well-integrated scheme, the whole can often be more profitable and interesting than the sum of the parts.

At university level, the most fruitful research fields often lie at the common boundaries of traditional disciplines. Thus, we have a proliferating range of new study areas such as business studies, mathematical biology, econometrics, computer-aided design, information technology, and often such new areas are partly constituted from modules of work from the traditional disciplines.

5. PROJECTS

The project can be a valuable vehicle for both enriching and extending the curriculum provided the project theme is well chosen and appropriate to the pupils concerned and rich in implied skills and curriculum links. It also needs careful preparation, and the kinds of material, apparatus and reference books likely to be required should be foreseen and available.

A middle school project on pyramids led to a lot of work on polyhedra and their nets, volumes, space filling, rigidity of structures and also to some work on Egyptian history, burial customs, slave labour, the Ptolemys, the treasures of the Pharaohs, beliefs about the afterlife and modern architecture (the Pompidou Centre). On the other hand, an ill-prepared project on the *omnium gatherum* theme of

'Transport' led to poor and trivial work.

By its nature a project generates enrichment around a central theme and usually throws up a need for new knowledge and new skills to be acquired.

Project or topic work in general and at its best involves the related language skills of listening, talking, reading and writing. It encourages the exercise of higher order reading skills – using a library, references, encyclopedias. It develops study skills of observation, note-taking, skimming and scanning, the planning and ordering of work and the basic notions of research using primary and secondary sources, documents, artefacts, maps and diagrams. It also exercises the general skills of analysis, synthesis and evolution – and sometimes results in empathy between pupils.

6. MODULAR LEARNING

We have already seen that for some new fields, modules of knowledge from traditional fields must be mastered, absorbed or transformed. In a sense, it is a process of extension from a simple structure to a more complex one formed by aggregation.

7. COMPETITIONS

To a degree the use of competitions to stimulate new learning and mastery lies somewhere between strategy and tactics. There is no doubt, however, that the mathematics in schools which participate in the mathematical olympiad or the City of London Polytechnic competitions or the Hans Woyda Interschool Competition, for example, are often more lively than elsewhere.

Tactics

As we have seen above there are long-term strategies which help us to enrich and extend teaching in a school. There are also temporary or short-term devices which can be employed to add variety or stimulus to classroom work. Most of the examples of strategies quoted above involve pupils working on their own, either on different individual tasks or projects, or all working singly upon the same theme. Most competitions also entail competitors operating as individuals. But in industry and research it is more usual nowadays for people to work in teams. Why, therefore, should students not work together co-operatively in twos, threes or even larger groups? Indeed, one round of the Hans Woyda competition mentioned above is a series of team challenges.

Clearly, the nature of the task determines to some extent the team. In an interschool competition, each school will clearly pick its ablest pupils. The International Olympiad teams also work and score together. And indeed, competitions apart, it is often beneficial for the able to work together.

HOMOGENEOUS ABILITY GROUPS
In activities such as the school choir, the school string quartet, the first soccer team, the chess team we find pupils of higher and roughly comparable abilities working and playing together. It can be exhilarating to sit in on a group of able youngsters sparking off ideas against one another. Each is on his or her toes. The joint outcome is sometimes much more fruitful than the sum of their individual efforts. Several such examples of noteworthy team efforts in mathematics are described in Chapter 6, pages 74–78 of *Teaching Able Children* by Tom Marjoram in this series.

Often, homogeneous ability groups are also contemporary by age, for example where a chronological organisation exists with ability sets in mathematics, science, modern languages, etc across each year group. But such groups *need* not be of equal age. Choirs and chess teams seldom are but it is perfectly acceptable to organise, as at least one school does, a 'zoom club' in mathematics. This meets twice a week with the head and draws able mathematicians from all year groups for the sole purpose of solving difficult mathematical problems. Some pupils like to work with their contemporaries but frequently mixed age groups form spontaneously.

MIXED ABILITY GROUPS
There is also something to be said for pairing able and less able pupils to work together from time to time. Often the abler takes the lead but learns much from having to think and find clear ways of conveying his thoughts. The less able also often learn better from a fellow student than from a teacher.

There are also many group tasks which do not need students of similar ability. I think of a Canadian school in which a team of pupils ran a small office stationery business for the local public. They produced headed note paper, visiting cards, wedding invitations, etc. The able artists concentrated on layout, the better mathematicians organised the finance, the sole car driver delivered orders, two meticulously careful pupils set up the type, the stronger, more modestly endowed intellectually worked the press and did the heavier work. A similar 'school bridge project' was very successfully completed with the aid of egg-head designers and cheerful hewers of wood and diggers of foundations. Oundle public school contracts to produce computer programs for local businesses to specification. This also calls upon very diverse talents in the contract team.

WORK PLANNING

One of the most unusual and successful ploys or tactics to encourage enrichment and extension work is used in a Brisbane high school. The most able pupils are told in advance each month the regular syllabus work they must complete in that time. By finishing before 'contract date' they can 'win' time to work on self-choice research projects. Moreover, there is a fund from which travel, apparatus, materials and other consequent 'research' costs may be financed. At the time of my visit to the school the following investigations or 'extension projects' were in progress: studies of abstract nouns, word processing applications, wood lathe work, fish breeding, plant growing under controlled conditions, aeronautics of sails and aspects of photography.

CONTRACT WORK

We have already mentioned the Canadian team of students who set up a business service and the Oundle team who produced computer programs to order. The same ideas, where local unions and employers' federations permitted, have been used in schools in Sofia, Bulgaria, and in many other parts of the world.

In Bulgaria, periods of work experience can be very substantial and involve the student in new and challenging real life situations and actual jobs in industry and commerce. One young student worked and travelled as personal assistant to an impresario, making travel arrangements, theatre bookings, and engaging actors for plays over a period of several months.

Work experience in England is shorter but, if well planned, can offer a good deal of stimulus and enrichment and a dimension of reality to what was learned at school.

Another student taking economics, law and mathematics at school was attached to a bank and worked briefly in all departments during her work experience.

MATERIALS

Enriching and extending the curriculum entails acquiring and using a wide variety of materials and apparatus not usually required in the normal run of classroom work.

The teacher also needs a store of problems, ideas for projects and investigations. Ideally, these should relate quite specifically to the various levels of each core and foundation subject of the National Curriculum and should help to *inter-relate* them.

Such materials include work cards, lists, maps, plans, slides, tapes and videos. In Chapters 5–10 we describe in detail some of the many extension and enrichment experiments, materials and strategies already tried successfully and a few of those that might be used in future to match and adapt better the 'regulation issue' of the mandatory National Curriculum to the very varied and diverse needs of our pupils.

Chapter 5

What it Means
in Practice

In previous chapters we have discussed those circumstances in which a curriculum – *any* curriculum – may need to be extended and accelerated or enriched and elaborated for some students. In this chapter we focus upon the National Curriculum, imposed by the 1988 Education Reform Act upon English schools, in so far as the details are presently available.

We know already that between 5 and 16 all children, with a small percentage of specified exemptions, must, from September 1989, follow a curriculum of three core subjects and seven foundation subjects. Each of these subjects is subdivided into attainment targets which together form the total content of that subject study up to 16+. For English there are five separate attainment targets; for science there are 17. Each attainment target (AT) is layered into ten levels of attainment or achievement. Level 1 is the easiest level; level 10 is the hardest. Most children will reach level 6 or 7 by the age of 16. *Programmes of study* briefly suggest ways of teaching and learning which could lead to the achievement of these levels.

Assessments will be made of each pupil's progress and achievement at the ages of 7 (key stage 1), 11 (key stage 2), 14 (key stage 3) and 16 years (key stage 4). National assessments at 16 and GCSE can hardly differ radically in aims and contents but whether they will continue side by side or ultimately coalesce into a single, summative assessment at 16 has yet to be resolved.

Full details of what will be expected at each level in English, mathematics and science have already been published and are available from HMSO, or, in essence, from WS Fowler's *Implementing the National Curriculum* in this same series of handbooks.

Interim reports on the profiles or attainment targets proposed in history, geography and technology are also available. At the time of writing, so far there is no information at all on the other curriculum subjects nor on RE, but well before 1995 it is expected that the full details of what is to be taught and assessed at all levels of all ten subjects of the curriculum will be available.

If this appears to be prescriptive, limiting and too inflexible to allow much variation of the kind we have been advocating, it is only fair and certainly necessary to stress the following points.

The National Curriculum Orders lay down only *minimum* requirements for each core and foundation subject. The content may go beyond what is prescribed at each level of each AT. Thus, other subjects may also be taught where time, ability and resources permit. The National Curriculum subjects may also (many would say *should*) be inter-related through cross-curricular studies and project work.

The Orders do not lay down the time that must be spent, nor indeed the timing. Above all, they specify no particular methods or textbooks. There is no lock-step requirement such as the French *niveau de la classe* whereby a pupil must reach a *given* level at a certain age. Theoretically, at any rate, each pupil may progress up the levels at his or her natural learning pace.

Finally, the Act and Orders apply only to pupils in key stages 1 and 3 from September 1989. Should GCSE continue in its present or modified form it would appear that pupils must be free to *opt* to take certain core and foundation subjects in GCSE while continuing others on a more limited basis. Indeed, they may take subjects outside the National Curriculum range such as Latin, an extra science, economics, etc as GCSE choices.

Thus the Act permits, within its framework, considerable scope for personal classroom initiative. It will certainly provoke much rethinking of current school organisation and will not necessarily sound the death knell of subjects such as Greek, domestic science and motor vehicle engineering.

A variety of classroom strategies of the kind described in Chapter 4 and in Christine Gilbert and Michael Hart's book in this series (*Towards Integration: Special Needs in an Ordinary School*) will be very relevant to such school organisation debates. Group work, circus arrangements (whereby, for example, three groups of pupils each study one of three practical activities for a term in turn), games and simulation exercises, individual learning systems like SMILE, projects, quizzes, team-teaching, open-ended investigation and library research may become more widespread, apposite and suitable to the demands of the new curriculum set-up than formerly.

One weakness of the Act is that it enshrines no underlying, unifying theory of curriculum and it offers little in the way of basic philosophy. Indeed, there is not a great deal of evidence that the programmes in mathematics, English and science are co-ordinated, related or co-operatively devised. Essentially similar skills common to any two or all three areas do not appear at the same time or level. For example, work on co-ordinates appears in mathematics at level 4. It does not appear in the interim geography proposals as 'grid reference' until levels 5 and 6. The use of standard form whereby a large number such as 1234567.8 is expressed as 1.2345678×10^6 does not appear until level 7 in maths yet it is required as scientific notation from level 4. 'Read a temperature scale' appears at level 3 in mathematics whereas knowing how temperature is measured features at level 4 in science. On the other hand, the English report does refer freely to language use in science and mathematics and quotes many illuminating examples.

The design and technology programmes of study for various levels do carry numerous cross-references to related attainment targets in mathematics, English and science. Doubtless this cross-curricular view or flavour will arise more often as the programmes of further foundation subjects emerge, particularly if, as some believe, testing in the foundation subjects may have to become telescoped into cross-curricular tasks in order to save time and expense. The current nightmare scenario of 16-year-olds taking ten national assessment tests *and* up to nine or ten GCSE examinations in their final term is hardly sustainable.

Even so, such thinking falls far short of being a proper taxonomy or of providing a holistic view of knowledge. Such taxonomies have existed for many years. Peters wrote extensively on this, and Bloom's taxonomy (see Chapter 2) is well known. One quoted by WS Fowler in his book *Implementing the National Curriculum*, a companion volume in this series, lists the aesthetic, human and social, linguistic, logico-mathematical, physical, scientific, technological, moral and spiritual elements of the curriculum.

The DES Assessment of Performance Unit (APU) used a model which saw the work of schools as being concerned with linguistic development, mathematics/logical thinking, empirical/scientific thinking, physical development, aesthetic and creative development and personal and social development (including the spiritual, moral and ethical dimensions). Thus any or all of these ways of thinking might at one point or another occur or be required in any subject. Thus, for instance, there are mathematical, technological, ethical and even moral aspects of the operation of the Stock Market. Television advertising carries linguistic, economic, mathematical, aesthetic and ethical connotations at least.

It is precisely these cross-curricular topics, and indeed the very act of seeing relationships between all the core and foundation subjects of the National Curriculum, which offer some of the most fruitful ways of enriching and extending it. (Some of the existing projects and available resource materials of this cross-curricular kind are described in Chapter 9.)

There is, however, also a wealth of enrichment material within each individual subject area, some of which are listed in the Bibliography and in earlier chapters.

Using the environment

One of the least effective ways of learning, certainly as far as younger children are concerned, is to follow through, subject by subject and level by level, the separate programmes of the National Curriculum. At all stages those programmes need to be constantly related to personal environment and first-hand experience.

Children learn directly through their senses and only vicariously from films, TV, pictures, records, tapes, videotapes and printed material. It is quite right that they should learn about the aborigines from pictures, films and stories as few are likely to visit Australia and see these people for themselves. It is essential that they learn about the Romans and Greeks from pictures, books and archaeological remains because they cannot possibly have first-hand knowledge of people long dead. But to read second-hand accounts of people, places and things they could very well see for themselves is anti-educational. And yet this may happen all too often. Instead of leaving the classroom to see people, places and things, the child may find himself reading about them in a book or being told about them by a teacher.

Clearly this is contrary to all our declared aims. The pupil should be observing for himself at first hand. He should be collecting real data, classifying and measuring it, making and testing simple hypotheses. He should talk about, write about and record his own experiences. Whenever possible, these should be direct and not second-hand or vicariously acquired. Hence the crucial importance of the environment and the way the school uses it.

For the young child the immediate environment is all-important. As far as the school is concerned, speech, writing, recording, painting, modelling, counting and measuring activities all flow from the classroom and its immediate environment. Many stimuli and starting points lie in the classroom and are indeed deliberately provided by the teacher. These will include matching and sorting games; shells, nuts, counters and other structural apparatus for counting; water, sand and clay; paints, paper, reading books and so on.

But on occasion, even more valuable stimuli are to be found outside the classroom – animals, plants and trees in the school grounds, or unusual happenings and incidents which detract attention and are sometimes well worth watching and talking about. One remembers, for instance, the arrival of an elephant by train to join a travelling circus in a small English town. Very wisely the teacher rushed all the children outside to gaze in wonder as the mighty beast plodded past totally obedient to its tiny keeper. It is not difficult to imagine the conversation and painting inspired by that event!

Of course, with young children particularly, supervision is very important and environmental work is correspondingly limited, but as children grow older it becomes possible for them to make much greater use of the immediate environment by allowing them to carry out unsupervised assignments. Here are a few examples of activities which pupils between the ages of 7 and 11 have undertaken outside the classroom:

- direct measurement of various aspects of the school building, its length and breadth, perimeter and area of the playground
- indirect measurement (eg by scale drawing) of the height of the school tower, a nearby church tower, the width of a lake, etc
- study of the architecture of local timber frame houses, a nearby Norman church, a local Elizabethan moat house, etc
- historical research based on local museum or local church records and facsimile documents
- survey of types and distribution of flora, plants and trees in the school grounds
- a detailed study of local woodland
- a study/search for plants of medicinal value in the area which resulted in the discovery and documentation of 200 different varieties
- plotting bird territories in the school grounds
- studying the diets of birds, collecting and analysing owl pellets found in school grounds and nearby woods
- making and observing animal habitats in the school grounds
- constructing, stocking, maintenance and study of the school pond
- study visit to a local factory, power station, etc
- study visit to a nearby farm
- study visit to a nearby zoo
- study trip to a nearby chalk pit rich in meteorites, fossil remains and other geological specimens.

WHAT IT MEANS IN PRACTICE

So much for the immediate locality. Children of 11 are ready to go further afield. By this age they can comprehend not only their own school and its role in the locality but they can think of the region and the country. Indeed, if they are learning a second modern language they may well benefit from a visit or educational exchange abroad. By 10 or 11, children are certainly ready for long day trips to see, for example:

- a newly built construction of note
- a new bridge, cathedral or radio telescope, etc
- a historical monument, cathedral, castle, Roman excavation, etc
- a performance of a play in a famous theatre
- a concert by an orchestra and artists of note
- an exhibition of painting
- a ballet of note
- an agricultural show, and so on.

Or there may be visits involving sleeping away from home for a few days under canvas, or in school or hotel accommodation. Such visits may simply have a pleasurable, recreational or social purpose such as a school camp. Many UK schools arrange such camps, usually partly or wholly in holiday time. Alternatively, the pupils may go on a tour, cruise, skiing holiday etc.

But longer visits of this kind may have a clear educational purpose and when this is the case may well take place in term time. Examples include:

- a five-day or long weekend visit to a field centre, bird sanctuary or nature reserve
- an area of extraordinary geological or geographical interest, when plenty of time is necessary for making observations, collecting specimens and making notes.

Optimum use of the distant environment, either for the day visit or the longer stay, often depends upon careful preparation. The time is usually better spent if the children know what to expect, and have done some preparatory reading or seen some film or photographs. It is sometimes better, too, if they have some choice of what to study – a highly regimented 'questionnaire filling' troop round a library or museum can be most tedious and less inspiring than staying at school.

The point must now be made that it is not necessary to widen the environment continually as children grow older. It is also possible to use the immediate environment in increasingly greater depths.

Some things emerge from the environment more readily than others. For example, the size, colour, window and door shape and exterior ornamentation of a building are more obvious than the fact (if it is a fact) that its dimensions are in golden section ratio. Indeed, mathematical patterns in natural forms are also much less obvious than more visual and other sensual attributes. The quality of observation, wonder, analysis, associations that a child brings to any environmental object or situation should increase in sensitivity, depth and range as the child grows and thus the teacher should always see that the tasks set not only exercise acquired skills and consolidate knowledge but should tax partially acquired expertise and increase experience.

Summarising then, environment – natural and man-made, near and far – should be seen by the teacher as one of his or her richest teaching resources. Like all powerful tools it calls for informed and intelligent use and a few simple criteria should be borne in mind.

To take a party of pupils out of the classroom may present difficulties of timetabling and organisation. With all children, particularly young ones, it can increase the hazards of supervision. Finally, it can be very time-consuming. On the other hand, it is nearly always better to observe at first hand and to experience 'the real thing'. A balance between these pros and cons must be maintained. Sometimes the cost in time, or sheer inaccessibility, renders the use of the environment uneconomic or impracticable. Sometimes the 'environment' can be brought into the classroom instead of taking the pupils out. Although there is value in seeing such items in their natural setting, plants, twigs, fruits, flowers can sometimes be brought into the classroom instead of taking pupils out to see them. Indeed, some plants can be grown and some small animals can be kept in the classroom. Museums will also occasionally lend specimens for classroom use.

Critics of environmental work point to the possible waste of time involved, to the fact that at worst some children may wander aimlessly about, to the fact that not all children are likely to be equally affected by the same stimulus, and that organisation and supervision are more difficult than in the classroom and sometimes insufficient.

However, successful practice shows that well-planned environment work can be invaluable. The key words are PLANNING and PURPOSE. Whenever environmental work is contemplated its purpose must be clear – not only to the teacher but to the pupils as well. Often, too, such work needs careful planning; the children must know what to expect and what to look for. Some preparatory reading or film may help. If apparatus or instruments are required – field glasses, cameras, magnifiers, specimen boxes, stop-watches, plane-tables, clinometers, chains, tape measures, anemometers, etc – they should be available, prepared and checked for working order.

Finally, the teacher must be open-minded and prepared for the unusual for, with luck, the children will not only see what they expected, but may also see something quite unexpected. Or, on the second visit, the teacher may spot something he or she did not see before.

Indeed, it is this element of the unpredictable that lends excitement to well-organised environmental work and which gives the opportunity, not always possible in the classroom, for choice, adaptability and real enterprise. Never was it more important for pupils to have these opportunities for direct observation, honest, first-hand reportage and opinion, and independent enquiry. Everything in this chapter applies to all children. The gifted will simply react sooner, faster, more deeply, more vividly, and often more surprisingly! Creativity is the unique rearrangement of experience. Without first-hand environmental stimulus, creativity and the natural spirit of enquiry and adventure will be inhibited in even the most able.

This approach is one of the best ways of enriching and extending the curriculum – of adding muscle and flesh to the bare bones of the nationally prescribed list of topics to be learned. It is also the most natural way of relating and mutually reinforcing those separate subjects.

The DES Oxford research

One of the most significant and extensive pieces of research into curriculum enrichment and its effects was the DES/Oxford research of 1982–86.

The most able 10 per cent of third-form pupils in mathematics, English, physics and French from 12 varied Oxfordshire comprehensive schools were studied. The first part of the research was concerned with *identification* of the ablest 10 per cent in each subject by teacher choice and test selection, the agreement or otherwise between these two modes and the ways in which they could be reconciled.

The second part of the research, confined to mathematics, physics and English, was about the effects of certain enrichment materials upon the performances of these students as compared with the performances of control groups that did not use them.

The outcomes have been described fully elsewhere and in *Teaching Able Children* by Tom Marjoram in this series. Briefly in mathematics, there were improvements in teaching strategies, methods of solution and in the students' ability to make generalisations. In English, attitudes to self-motivated writing improved with increased ranges of reading and enthusiasm for it. In physics, several improvements in categories of experimental design were noticed.

In all three areas, all the selected students benefited; the teachers welcomed the materials but found they required careful preparation and some INSET, and short projects were preferred to longer-term projects and investigations. The latter reaction probably reflected the pupils' lack of confidence and inexperience in this more open and less prescribed way of working and most wished that they had started earlier and could continue the experiment longer.

In some schools the new material was not very different in flavour from the normal rich and varied teaching programme but in others it seemed to come as a welcome and stimulating contrast to the normal routines. As we have remarked earlier, one person's 'enrichment' is another's normal diet.

Of greatest interest in the context of this book are examples of the materials used in the DES/Oxford project.

THE ENGLISH MATERIALS
These included the following:

1. *Family*
An original writing assignment which involved students' investigations of their own great-grandparents and family trees – birth places, lifestyles, occupations and houses. Students researched family records and they interviewed and taped old people where possible. Some had grandparents who had been born in other countries and this led to some interesting accounts of travel, family crises and upheavals, and life in very different times and places.

2. *Riddley Walker*
A reading project which involved making sense out of nonsense, reading Burns and Carroll and other nonsense verse, a study of Anthony Burgess' illuminating review of Hoban's work and language and which led on to paraphrase and note-making.

3. *David Copperfield*
This book was compared with *Gulliver's Travels* as two examples of autobiographical technique. The students reflected upon childhood memory and its reliability and drew all manner of comparisons between these two and other autobiographies and, for example, between their own school and Dotheboys Hall. They looked at Swift's use of language to describe scale in, for example, the voyage to

Brobdingnag, the terrible vision of the Queen eating and the terrifying sizes of flies and other animals.

4. *Ways of speaking*

Three different recorded examples of speech by an aggrieved West Indian, an excited football commentator and someone with a languid, 'upper crust' drawl were studied for cues about location, occupation and social class. Vocabulary, grammar and syntax were also examined. Students then made other examples of recorded speech from willing interviewees. They looked at two different sets of speeches. In the first examination they recorded different people talking about the same topic or event; in the second they recorded the same person speaking with or addressing very different audiences such as friendly conversation with individual contemporaries, children, strangers, business associates and also with small and large groups in social chat, educational or business seminars, lessons, public addresses, etc.

In both cases they analysed speed, volume, restraint, emphasis, abbreviation, idiom, slang, vocabulary and syntax form. Some also mastered techniques of phonetic transcription for recording heard remarks and speech extracts.

THE PHYSICS MATERIALS

These took the form of practical investigations and mini research topics.

1. The first investigation was to ascertain whether water that's been heated and cooled freezes faster than ordinary cold water.

    The work involved free discussion on how to tackle the question, a literature review of whether any other scientists had already studied this or related questions, a precise formulation of the questions to be addressed, experimental strategy, choice of apparatus, recording of results, and practical work necessary. At the end results had to be interpreted, conclusions drawn and a report produced.

2. A second investigation involved rotating discs with coloured sectors. This led on to a study of colours, light, stereoscopic vision and the function of the human eye. It involved prediction, observation and explanation.

3. Another investigation started with a given variety of rubber suckers and suction pads and the question was asked 'which is the "best"

rubber sucker?' This entailed defining 'best' and reformulating and 'unpacking' the question.

4. Yet another exercise presented a number of simple circuit diagrams with batteries, lamp bulbs and ammeters in various branches and asked questions about the currents through various bulbs and the readings in different ammeters. Relating this to experimental results the students were led to deduce notions about current flow and Kirchhoff's Laws. One of the final challenges was to write a teaching scheme to help other third-formers understand simple series circuits!

5. One of the more unusual science enrichment studies entitled 'Science Fact from Science Fiction', focused upon good science fiction such as *Tales from the White Hart* by Arthur Clarke and asked the students to react to such stories, analysing what was stimulating about them. This led on to classic science fiction which had indeed predicted the future by, for example, HG Wells, George Orwell and Jules Verne.

THE MATHEMATICS MATERIALS
There is a wealth of information about puzzles, problems and project of all kinds in mathematics, and the Oxfordshire students were certainly encouraged to refer to these. (Some of these are listed in the Bibliography.) The students were also given problems to tackle.

1. One was about palindromic numbers (numbers which, like 171, read the same forward or backwards) and car speedometers. Students investigated the number of palindromic numbers that could appear on a six-digit milometer dial and the probability of a palindromic number appearing when the car next stopped.

2. Students investigated the magic square:

7	10	13	0
12	1	6	11
2	15	8	5
9	4	3	14

3. They researched matrices of the following kind:

$$\begin{pmatrix} a & b \\ c & d \end{pmatrix}^2 = \begin{pmatrix} a^2 & b^2 \\ c^2 & d^2 \end{pmatrix}$$

For example,

$$\begin{pmatrix} 2 & 5 \\ 0 & 3 \end{pmatrix}^2 = \begin{pmatrix} 2^2 & 5^2 \\ 0^2 & 3^2 \end{pmatrix}$$

4. Another very rich investigation was introduced by the simple question, 'Can you cut out an 8-inch square cake into seven squares?' Extensions of this flowed from changing the size of the cake to produce seven squares and alternatively listing other sets of squares into which an 8 by 8 square could be cut. 'Squares' is a level 3 topic in the National Curriculum and it can be developed endlessly.

Continuing the above theme, we could have asked for different ways of expressing 8^2 as the sum of a set of seven squares. One solution to this is $8^2 = 6^2 + 3^2 + 3^2 + 2^2 + 2^2 + 1^2 + 1^2$, but in this case, squares of side 6,3,3,2,2,1,1 *cannot* be assembled like a jigsaw into a square of side 8.

It recalls Lagrange's theorem that every positive integer is a sum of four or fewer perfect squares. For example:

$$
\begin{aligned}
6 &= 2^2 + 1^2 + 1^2 \\
79 &= 7^2 + 5^2 + 2^2 + 1^2 \\
80 &= 8^2 + 4^2
\end{aligned}
$$

The set of numbers 100, 110, 120, 130 (ie $10 \times (10+n)$ for $n = 0,1,2,3$ ...) is an interesting subset of this. One can discover which of these can be expressed as four or fewer squares numerically and which of these rectangles can be sectioned into four or fewer squares.

Ultimately this leads us to some interesting jigsaw puzzles such as:

$$
\begin{aligned}
112^2 = {} & 2^2 + 4^2 + 6^2 + 7^2 + 8^2 + 9^2 + 11^2 + 15^2 + 16^2 + 17^2 + 18^2 \\
& + 19^2 + 24^2 + 25^2 + 27^2 + 29^2 + 33^2 + 35^2 + 37^2 + 42^2 + 50^2
\end{aligned}
$$

both numerically *and* geometrically!

If n can become a non-integer we get some interesting partitions into infinite sets of squares. Consider, for example:

$$
\begin{aligned}
10(10+n) = {} & 10^2 + n^2 + (n-10)^2 + (2n-10)^2 + (3n-20)^2 + (5n-30)^2 \\
& + (8n-50)^2 + (13n-80)^2 + (21n-130)^2 + (34n-210)^2
\end{aligned}
$$

It is interesting to see how these build up and to consider the limiting value of n for which the process actually works (see Figure 5.1).

5. Another interesting investigation is into the pattern:

$$
\begin{aligned}
1 \times 1 &= 1 \\
11 \times 11 &= 121 \\
111 \times 111 &= 12321
\end{aligned}
$$

and ultimately such products as, for example,

777777×999999

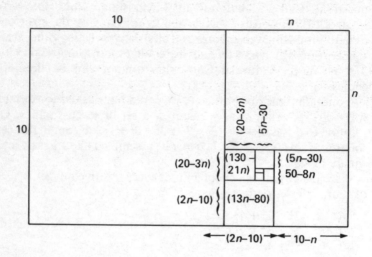

Figure 5.1

6. In one of the investigations, students were given figures about populations, live birth rates and death rates at certain times in the past and were asked to estimate future population statistics.

7. One very interesting section was about *ancient* problems. For example, an old Hindu problem states that while three watchmen were guarding an orchard a thief climbed in and stole some apples. On his way out he met each watchman one after the other. To each he gave half the apples he had and an additional two. He finally escaped with one apple. The question is to find how many apples he stole (N).

This is a good exercise in equation building. For after the first encounter he has $N - \left(\dfrac{N}{2} + 2 \right)$ or $\dfrac{N}{2} - 2$.

After the second $\left(\dfrac{N}{2} - 2 \right) - \left\{ \dfrac{1}{2} \left(\dfrac{N}{2} - 2 \right) + 2 \right\}$ or $\dfrac{N}{4} - 3$.

After the third $\left(\dfrac{N}{4} - 3 \right) - \left\{ \dfrac{1}{2} \left(\dfrac{N}{4} - 3 \right) + 2 \right\}$ or $\dfrac{N}{8} - \dfrac{7}{2}$ which $= 1$.

There were many other investigations involving, for example, computers, market research, games, the strange billiard table (of SMILE fame), population prediction, the Rhind Papyrus, calendar problems, Diophantine equations, and postage stamp denominations. In Chapter 8 we indicate some sources of help in the form of organisations which may be able to supply curriculum enrichment or extension material or which organise conferences and produce papers and journals on the subject. Chapter 9 then describes some of the other packs and materials already available.

Chapter 6

Who Provides?

It has been established in earlier chapters that the needs of more able children are complex and diverse. Therefore, if an effective response is to be found a wide variety of individuals will have to play a part. Some of these people will not deal directly with the children but will be part of the structure and planning; others will have a major role in the children's day-to-day development.

Provision for enrichment and extension involves:

- the LEA
- the school
- the class teacher
- the parents
- the wider community.

The role of the local education authority

If provision for enrichment and extension is to be effective it requires a co-ordinated response from the LEA. It is time-consuming for schools to find resources to meet an individual's needs and this time is unlikely to be allocated against a background of competing needs in school. Equally, more able children will be discovered and more potential fulfilled if schools are encouraged to enrich and extend the curriculum. However, this will be done most effectively by sharing knowledge and expertise across schools and a co-ordinated LEA response is needed to facilitate this. The LEA can therefore help schools to respond to the needs of exceptional individual children and at the same time encourage a broader approach at curriculum development level.

At a time when curriculum development and differentiation are key educational issues it is important that LEAs should promote this approach as an effective response. An enriched and extended curriculum will make effective provision for a wider variety of children and this should be an integral part of all school planning and evaluation. Whole-school projects such as self-evaluation and records of achievement should all reflect the presence of an enriched and extended curriculum. This considered curriculum response will be of enormous benefit to schools in implementing the National Curriculum. It will allow children to work at a number of different levels, as envisaged by the National Curriculum, while for the most part remaining within their age-related classes. The LEA can provide assistance for schools both in this curriculum development role and in meeting the special needs of individuals by making expertise and facilities available to its schools. In comparison with many other educational support systems this one is reasonably cheap since it does not require substantial additional staffing in schools but rather a small amount of staffing at central level.

The areas where the LEA might most usefully play a role are in:

(a) inservice
(b) special needs
(c) resources
(d) research.

(a) INSERVICE
As in all curriculum areas the LEA has a vital role to play in providing inservice training for curriculum enrichment and extension. Schools have to be made aware of the need to respond effectively to children with ability or talent and given some indication how to achieve this. Aspects which could usefully be considered include:

- managing and organising the classroom for enrichment and extension
- differentiation within the National Curriculum
- extension and enrichment ideas in specific subject areas
- pilot schemes to explore and encourage good practice
- work in music, sport and the arts
- a magazine to disseminate examples of good practice
- linking enrichment and extension to other school and LEA initiatives.

In addition to work in and with schools, part of the inservice role is concerned with liaising with subject advisers, phase advisers and project leaders to establish a working response to enrichment and extension across a wide variety of fields. For example, more able children where English is not the first language, or equal opportunities for bright girls. Many of these issues remain untouched in education although it is recognised that work may need to be done. It may be, for example, that enriching and extending the curriculum for all has major benefits for girls, but this needs to be explored in the context of other equal opportunities work being undertaken.

(b) SPECIAL NEEDS

Some authorities operate a system whereby exceptional children are identified by schools and provision is made for them through the special needs support teams. This is a manifestation of the idea that talented children have special needs in the widest sense. In some cases each support team has one member whose remit is particularly concerned with exceptional children and in others each team member works with a small number of schools and deals with children across the whole spectrum of special needs.

Both of these approaches have certain advantages. In the latter system the special needs teacher knows the school and children well and the exceptional child's needs are met within the normal framework of the school. In the former the special needs teacher is likely to have greater expertise and therefore be more effective in finding a suitable response. Whichever working method is adopted it is essential that the personnel involved have access to regular inservice training at county level to increase their expertise and share professional concerns.

The role of special needs teachers in respect of exceptional children may well differ from their other work. It is likely that the majority of their time will be spent with the child's teacher assisting in planning, evaluating and profiling the child rather than in small group teaching. They can help the teacher and the school to make the most effective use of outside resources and personnel and also have the advantage of being able to maintain a link with the child throughout her schooling and so facilitate continuity. There may be occasions when the child works with the special needs teacher as part of a group doing enrichment or extension activities but it is unlikely that the special needs teacher will teach the child on, for example, a weekly basis, as is more commonly their approach to the less able children. This is because integration into the class is a high priority and while all children benefit from small group work and adult attention, in the case of talented children the advantages of withdrawal by special needs teachers are not so great as to overcome the disadvantages.

(c) RESOURCES

Useful resources for schools are materials and personnel. In both cases it is time-consuming for a school to draw up lists of these and they can usually be created at a central level and then used by a wide variety of schools.

Materials are often made available through an *enrichment centre*. It is very expensive for a school to buy materials which may only be of use to a limited number of children or in some cases a single child and so some authorities collect together suitable materials and hold them in a library base. These bases usually lend materials for about half a term and are staffed by a librarian who will advise and assist teachers in their choices. In some large shire counties the base also distributes a smaller range of materials which is held in local teachers' centres or other similar professional venues.

These centres fulfil a number of useful roles:

- They draw together high quality materials which may be of use in enrichment and extension activities.
- They encourage a school to think about enrichment and extension and the role it may play in their planning.
- They can serve as a central focus in the LEA's exceptional child provision with support personnel working from the centre.
- They can be a venue for inservice training in this field.
- They can display the results of successful extension and enrichment activities.

Often enrichment or extension requires the use of expertise beyond that available in school, especially in small schools. Locating suitable personnel can be difficult and time-consuming and therefore it is very useful to schools if a *central register of personnel* can be created. People on such a register may come from a variety of sources:

- individuals known to have a particular interest or hobby
- representatives of local societies
- individuals in higher education institutions willing to work in schools
- representatives of the LEA interested in working with more able children in their own subject area
- representatives from industry.

It is important that a list of this type is serviced by someone within the LEA both to keep it up to date and to disseminate examples of successful projects. Where contacts have proved less successful it is important to establish reasons and so avoid similar occurrences. In addition, it is crucial that individuals on the list, and other interested agencies, have a recognised point of contact within the LEA if this type of facility is to be used effectively.

Able children generally make good use of enrichment opportunities which originate from outside the school and a school-initiated contact with a local society or interest group may well lead to a life-long involvement for a child. Reserved children often find it easier to make social contact in an environment where people have a common interest rather than a more informal situation so the opportunity is doubly beneficial.

(d) RESEARCH

Much of the policy or strategies advocated by LEAs are a response to educational research findings. The LEA can assist schools both by undertaking its own research in this field and by keeping abreast of other work done in this country and abroad. NACE has a strong research committee which can inform about national research and is also linked to the World Council for Gifted and Talented Children for a more international view.

Many LEAs undertake small-scale action research, and curriculum enrichment and extension are worthwhile areas to consider.

It is obvious, therefore, that much of the work undertaken at LEA level involves co-ordinating and facilitating. Linking schools with suitable ideas, people and resources and liaising with other members of the advisory teams in exploring how enrichment and extension opportunities can be created in respect of a large variety of other initiatives. In addition, it is to encourage and facilitate the development of suitable responses to the needs of exceptional children in schools, to evaluate their success and to disseminate examples of good practice. If these roles are to be satisfactorily accomplished then an authority needs at the very least one person at adviser or advisory teacher level with enrichment and extension as his or her concern.

The role of the school

The school is of course central in providing for all children. Its role operates in two ways:

- It provides an environment where children's abilities can be discovered and nurtured.
- It then structures its curriculum to meet the needs of the individual.

Neither of these ways can be worked successfully in isolation. If the school only operates a 'knee jerk' response to individuals, that is, developing suitable programmes of work to meet the needs of a child or children who display signs of high ability, then the approach is fragmentary. It is very time-consuming for the school and the class teacher both in terms of planning and monitoring and the child is likely to feel isolated from the main group. The ability will not in general disappear and so this type of individual approach would need to be sustained throughout the child's schooling. Much teacher time would be involved for limited gain. Indeed, if this system were in operation for a number of children in the class it would quickly become unworkable.

In addition, this system only comes into operation if the teacher is aware of the child's special ability. It does nothing for covertly able children and relies greatly on the teacher's identification skills. While we know these to be reasonably good:

Percentage of 'A' group pupils nominated by teachers

	English	French	Physics	Maths
All schools	80.8	61.4	53.7	76.2

(Denton/Postlethwaite, 1985)

they are by no means infallible and even if such a success rate were maintained it would still leave potential undiscovered.

Equally, if a school has a recognised approach for identifying and providing for exceptional children then it will only be truly effective if it is flexible enough to take account of the needs of the individual. A framework which encourages curriculum enrichment and extension is therefore essential but it must be tailored to take account of individual needs.

Some schools incorporate this type of framework into a formalised school policy. Figure 6.1 shows the school policy document for Holyport CE Primary School. Here the aims in respect of able children are incorporated into the general aims of the school. It is interesting to note the third school aim: 'To recognise each child as an individual, to develop self-discipline and help them realise their potential.' This places the needs of the more able firmly as an integral aspect of responding to the needs of all children – the well-known Belle Wallace (1983) quote: 'Gifted provision for all children not provisions for gifted children.'

The second part of the policy lists a number of general points which the school aims to incorporate into its curriculum. The first two points, to appoint a member of staff and to meet needs within the mainstream

Figure 6.1: *Policy document for the able child*
(Holyport CE Primary School)

Aims of the School

'Our main aim is to draw out the special talents and aptitudes of each individual child'.

'To help pupils to develop lively, inquiring minds, the ability to question and argue rationally and to apply themselves to relevant tasks and physical skills.'

'To recognise each child as an individual, to develop self-discipline and help them realise their potential.'

Keeping these aims in mind, provision for the able should be seen as an aspect of provision for *all* children, as an integral part of equal opportunity for all pupils.

There are several aspects of exceptional ability that need recognition and should be taken into account.

- physical ability
- skill in visual and performing arts
- mechanical ingenuity
- leadership and social awareness
- high intelligence
- creativity (permeating each aspect).

Therefore, the aims of the school for the able child are:

- To appoint a member of staff to lead and co-ordinate work relating to the able child.
- To meet the needs of advanced development within the mainstream curriculum.
- To provide a range of extension material that will meet the demand for enrichment within the curriculum. To incorporate intellectual challenge through the *quality* rather than the quantity of work.
- To provide self-initiated and self-directed learning that will encourage the able child to develop the attitude that knowledge is worth pursuing.
- To prepare them for an understanding of one's relationships to persons and society.
- To develop a skills-based curriculum that will provide the necessary stimulating work.

curriculum, are essentially organisational undertakings. They recognise the need to provide and state how these will be tackled at a whole-school level. Points three, four and six address the learning process and outline briefly the types of strategy the school will use. Point five recognises social needs and gives them equal status with the child's intellectual needs.

This document does not then attempt to explain in detail its school provision but outlines its general philosophy against which all curriculum planning takes place.

A document of this type fulfils two functions. Firstly, it provides a philosophical backdrop against which teachers can do their planning and against which new teachers to the school (and parents) can gain an understanding of what the school is seeking to do. Secondly, and perhaps more importantly in some ways, is the act of developing the policy. Whole-school discussion and exploration of the issues involved are the best way to effect real change. Professional concerns and practical considerations can be discussed and this will hopefully lead to a consensus view. If continuity of approach is to be achieved then it is important that the issues are thoroughly discussed, otherwise what might look wonderful in school documentation can prove non-existent in the classroom!

So far then the school has discussed and documented its philosophical approach but this is only one step towards providing a suitably enriched and extended curriculum. Much more discussion will be needed if the school is to find ways to put these aims into practice. Certainly the following issues still need to be discussed:

- What exactly is enrichment and extension and how do we provide it (see Chapters 2 and 3)?
- How can we keep track of what we are providing and for whom?
- What are we going to do about children with exceptional ability in one or more areas?
- If process is just as important as content does our record-keeping take account of it?
- When we discuss specific subject areas should we look at the more able?
- If we incorporate a system which allows extension how do we facilitate good transition to the next school?

These are all important issues and likely to be the subject of heated professional discussion. Some possible answers and suggestions are to be found in other parts of this book as well as in other books on this subject (see Bibliography) but every school is different in terms of its organisation, personnel and existing teaching policy and so must explore for itself.

As was mentioned earlier in this chapter most LEAs provide some support for their schools in this field. Either through a nominated individual on the staff or through the head teacher schools need to find out what is available and how they can best use it. It is, for example, no use having an enrichment centre 25 miles from the school and expecting each member of staff to use it personally – they won't. However, the centre could still serve a useful function by:

- ordering from a catalogue with one teacher collecting and delivering
- organising collection and delivery through a 'cluster'
- arranging to have a variety of sample materials in school for a week and having a whole staff visit to the centre to familiarise colleagues with what is available so that particularly useful materials could be purchased by the school or cluster.

Much of the provision at both LEA and school level is about co-ordination. Therefore, to make the best use of available opportunities each school needs someone with able children as their responsibility. They will look at everything and everyone who comes into school in terms of how they might be used to extend or enrich the curriculum and will therefore spot unusual opportunities which could have potential.

The role of the class teacher

So far in this chapter we have moved from the general to the specific. We have looked at LEA provision and school provision but obviously the person with the most direct role is the class teacher. All the work done at LEA and school level is an attempt to respond to the needs of and give support to the class teacher, for it is his or her expertise which will in the final analysis allow children to fulfil their potential.

Providing for a wide variety of children in the classroom is not easy. That is why some schools put their brightest children up to the next class and others deny the existence of their able children altogether. Bright children can be precocious, challenging, ask very awkward questions, be intolerant of others and difficult to integrate into the class. They can equally be quiet, retiring, never answer questions unless asked directly and make it difficult to ascertain the level of their ability. Therefore, in providing a suitable curriculum it is helpful to keep some general principles at the forefront of the mind:

- Try to keep a sense of humour.
- Provide the best you can and don't be too concerned if it doesn't always work out.
- Be prepared to be flexible and build on your success.

- Don't try to know all the answers; enjoy the realisation that some children know more and can do it better than you.
- Remember that as an adult you will always have the experience to *nurture* the child's potential even if her ability is superior to your own.
- Look to enrich and extend the curriculum whenever opportunities are available for as many of the children as you can.
- Aim high for all children and reward progress, but do not pressure children with unreasonable expectations.
- Enjoy yourself because that enhances the children's enjoyment.

Class teachers need to become skilled at recognising and providing for potential. This is a continuous circle: if you provide then you uncover more children for whom you then provide, and so on. The curriculum needs to allow for discovering ability and then using it. Therefore, the main roles of the teacher in curriculum terms are:

- To provide as wide a variety of opportunities within each subject as possible.
- To provide opportunities for tasks at differing levels of difficulty.
- To match those tasks to appropriate children.
- To have a clear view of children's attainments, not just in content and concept terms but to profile, for example, good ability in problem-solving or information retrieval.
- To find opportunities within the curriculum for children to tackle tasks in whatever way they are most successful, ie not all work will be done in isolation but using groups and teams. Not just written recording but also tapes, verbal and pictorial presentations.
- To make provision for the more able an integral part of general planning rather than a 'bolt on' afterthought.

Of course, the curriculum is only part of the class teacher's role. He or she also ensures that children are happy and fulfilled members of the class. This will be partially achieved if the children's intellectual needs are met but their social needs also have to be taken into account. Many bright children need a special relationship with their teacher. They are often sensitive and thrive if the relationship with their teacher is good but withdraw if they feel uneasy or undervalued. Some exceptional children find it difficult to conform to school norms but an understanding teacher can often help them come to terms with the demands of school. It is helpful to recognise that talented children do have special needs in the broadest sense and that as teachers we should not feel any guilt about time spent with them.

Many class teachers also find they spend unusually large amounts of time with the parents of exceptional children. This is partly because the child is probably experiencing a curriculum which differs at least in some respects from those of his peers, and which therefore requires some explanation. Parents are naturally anxious if their child is not

---

Figure 6.2: *How to help children fulfil their potential*

If children are to fulful their potential they need to:

- have a secure environment in which they feel happy to display ability
- experience failure
- relax and have fun
- have a person who understands their strengths and weaknesses
- have firm but sensitive handling
- know that they may ask searching questions and expect a considered response
- get lots of praise
- have a good relationship between home and school
- be recognised as an individual with special needs but within the normal classroom environment
- undertake stimulating work at higher cognitive levels
- have opportunities which really challenge and stretch their abilities
- solve and devise problems at an appropriate level
- be able to discuss meaningfully with the teacher
- learn to evaluate their work and become self-critical
- know that quality, not quantity, is of value
- be encouraged to speculate and hypothesise
- be given short-term attainable goals
- be taught relevant skills but not be called upon to do irrelevant practice
- be encouraged to take responsibility for organising aspects of their own work
- work in a team
- value the skills and aptitudes of others
- learn to co-operate and seek the help and advice of others where appropriate
- learn acceptable social behaviour
- know that they are valued not just for their abilities
- develop a variety of interests
- have their development profiled effectively
- have continuity of provision throughout their schooling
- have some opportunity to work with others of similar ability.

---

doing the same as other children and need to understand the benefits of a differentiated approach. They need to know what the teacher hopes the child will achieve in certain tasks so that they too can see and reinforce progress. Sometimes the teacher finds him or herself reassuring parents if the child has reached a plateau in learning or has not reacted in the expected way to opportunities made available. It is sometimes difficult to be the parent of an exceptional child because they can behave differently from most children. Parents hope that the school will make effective provision for their child because they may not know what effective provision should be.

If the teacher works closely with the parents to make a professional response to the child's needs then many parents are very supportive. If, however, this kind of time is not allocated, parents can begin to feel that the school is not making effective provision and seek out-of-school algebra lessons or similar, with all the resultant home/school friction, which can be especially damaging for sensitive children.

In short, the class teacher provides a suitable academic and social climate to enable the child to fulfil his potential. Figure 6.2 suggests how this might be achieved. An enriched and extended curriculum allows the class teacher to meet those needs.

The role of the parent

Many books have been written for and by the parents of more able children (see Bibliography) and, in addition, the National Association for Gifted Children was formed by interested parents. It emerges both from the literature as well as from talking to parents that many parents find themselves in conflict with their children's schools. The main reasons seem to be:

- The parent thinks the child has potential but the school does not.
- The school does not think it appropriate to make any special provision for exceptional children.
- The parents think the child could achieve more highly but is not given the opportunities in school.
- The parents do not think the child is given the 'right' kind of work while the school thinks that parents want narrow acceleration which it won't provide.

Whatever the reason, which is often a combination of the above, the relationship is tense and strained and is not helpful for parents, school or, most importantly, the child. It has to be said at this point that some schools *are* unresponsive and that some parents *are* unreasonably aggressive but, in general, with effort on both sides, it is possible to evolve an effective relationship.

Consider then the reasons for conflict listed above. Firstly, *does the child have exceptional potential?* Schools often feel that they should decide this rather than parents. In some ways this is a little unreasonable since parents know their children better than teachers but then again teachers see far more children in general and therefore feel better able to decide who is considerably above the average. Personally, I do not think that this is an issue worthy of argument. In England, if children are said to be more able, this does *not* mean that they will go to a different school or in general be in a different class, it just means that they *might* have the ability to do well in one or a combination of fields. Therefore, if any party feels the child may have potential then the opportunities should be made available. It is not a case of who is right or wrong; if a child does better than the school expected, they should feel pleased. If the child proves unable to take advantage of the opportunities presented then parents must not see the child as failing but value what has been achieved.

Perhaps if opportunities were offered in another area the outcome may be different but in any case performance is a different thing from potential and research shows that children who convert potential into performance usually have caring, supportive but not pressurising parents.

Should the school make special provision? From an educational viewpoint it is difficult to justify the argument that schools should not make provision for exceptional children. Schools which adhere to this philosophy do so out of a misguided sense of egalitarianism. They see bright children as already advantaged and in a climate of diminishing resources feel they warrant little time or consideration. Any deeper examination of the issue shows that this attitude leads to underachievement, disruptive pupils and low standards. Bright children need challenge and stimulation, otherwise they use their talents in less constructive ways!

Fortunately, this attitude is in decline. The Education Reform Act and National Curriculum documents refer to the need to provide appropriately for more able or gifted pupils and this is a reflection of present educational views. More worrying perhaps for the parents is the tight financial pressures on schools because, while acknowledging the need to provide for the more able, schools see other issues as more pressing. Here parents can play a useful role in raising awareness at national and LEA level, as well as using the governorship role to enhance provision.

Figure 6.3: *Questions for parents to ask themselves*

What is your home like every day for your children?

What is the atmosphere like? What is the feeling tone: tense, relaxed, chaotic, orderly, structured?

What is your attitude? Are you usually happy, positive, available, responsive? Aloof, angry, annoyed, harried and hurried?

How do you talk to one another in your home? What's the routine, the daily schedule?

How do you respond to daily crises, from spilled milk, on up to the policeman at the door and beyond?

Has everything become a crisis for you?

Can you recognise the difference between a minor problem and a very difficult, long-range one? Do you tend to ignore and hurry problems?

Is the television, radio, stereo, a constant background of sound? Is there time to talk to one another? How many times a day do you say 'Just a minute', 'Don't bother me now', 'See me later'?

Does your family live together well?

Would your children's answers be the same as yours?

What kind of parent do you think you are?

Is it the same perception that your children have of you? Remember: what is perceived *is*.

Have they ever told you what they think of your parenting style? When they do, is it often in *anger* and so an exaggerated, distorted description and perception?

Do you think you talk too much, give too many directions, give too many answers?

Do you usually say **NO** as an immediate response to your children's requests, without really thinking through the possibility? Do you choose your **nos** carefully, for the important things?

Do you think you might be in the habit of laying a guilt trip on your children, returning again and again to behaviours that should be long forgotten?

Do you *resent* your role as the parent of a gifted child or children? **Why me?** Or are you in awe of the role you have?

Is your whole existence tied to your child's successes and failures?

Should the child be given more opportunities? If a school is enriching and extending then opportunities will be made available to the widest possible body of children. The usual reason for this not occurring is that the teacher does not want the child to be faced with a task he is unable to tackle. This is a question of climate. It is good and healthy to take risks provided that failure is seen as part of the learning experience. All children need to fail sometimes and to learn to cope with failure. Many tasks can in any case be offered without failure but with relative degrees of success – possible solution, practical solution, elegant solution!

Does the child do the right kind of work? Here is a common arena for conflict. Parents do not know as much about education as teachers and tend to confuse skills acquisition with learning. If the child can add she should move on to subtraction; if she reads easy books, she must borrow from the class above. Obviously skills acquisition is part of learning but only a part. If a child is good at acquiring a certain type of skill it does not need significantly more emphasis but some room to explore other issues. Schools have not always taken the time to share their knowledge and aims with parents and would be prudent to do so rather more.

What, then, can parents do to ensure that their child gains the most from schooling? Much work has been done on this in America. Ella Mae Gogel, National Chairwoman of the Parent Committee of the Association for Talented and Gifted (TAG); Council for Exceptional Children, advocates supporting the school and establishing a warm relationship at home. In Figure 6.3 she asks some interesting questions which *this* parent found thought-provoking. In respect of school she asks: 'When did you last tell your school they were doing something well?'

Parents rarely visit school to be enthusiastic but appear swiftly if they are unhappy. So the parent's role must be to provide a warm, supportive environment for the child at home and to work with the school in providing a good education. If the school and parents have a friendly relationship with respect on both sides then any problems which arise will be more easily resolved.

Help from outside the school

Traditionally, schools have used members of their local community to add an additional dimension to the child's school experiences. This has an important role in curriculum enrichment and could usefully be extended. Also, schools can look to other outside agencies for help with curriculum enrichment and extension.

Firstly, most schools use anyone that they can find who has an interest or expertise in a project they are undertaking. Therefore, the local builder may visit or take the children out on to site when working on houses and homes, or the school dentist may give a talk when 'our bodies' is the termly topic. This is one level of using outside expertise. It could be improved through the use of a local register of interested people as suggested earlier in the chapter. Often, as a teacher, one only becomes aware of an individual's interest after the topic is completed. Parents will mention weeks later at parents' evening, 'You could have asked my father to talk about the railways, he did so and so . . . .' This kind of information could usefully be stored for later use.

We are all aware of the value of outside input in terms of enthusiasm and expertise and the effect it has upon the children. High quality work can and does emerge as well as a wider understanding of the world in which we live. Older members of the community can feel valued if invited into school and relationships between individual children and older citizens can develop. Often children take maximum advantage of these opportunities and they are a good way to motivate those whose general response to school is not as we might hope.

Expertise can also be made available through dance, music, art and drama. Many schools realise the value of supplying a good role model. Authors, musicians, ballet dancers, etc are invited to school so that children can appreciate both what is possible and how it was achieved. It can be inspirational for many children to hear music, played well, at close quarters for the first time, and may well encourage them to take up an instrument. To some extent schools take up offers made to them, so the types of opportunity are uneven. It might be useful for schools to consider what they would like to offer, rather than what is available, and if necessary seek it out. For example, it is not common to see exhibitions or talks by modern artists in school but children could have a wider understanding if they were introduced to artists' work in the same way as authors' work.

This idea of showing what is possible is seldom extended to the academic field. Many university researchers work on subjects which are fascinating for everyone. Usually the image of the absentminded professor is totally erroneous and the research or university teacher can often present work in an enthusiastic and interesting way. For example, the astrophysicist who brings along his mobile planetarium or the zoologist who talks about animal behaviour. Some people like giving talks and presentations at school more than others so again it is useful to develop a list of interested personnel.

So far we have discussed using people from beyond the school to give talks and presentations. However, this is only one role which they may play and many people who do not feel able or willing to contribute in this way have much to offer the school. One way is through increasing teachers' skills and knowledge. Traditionally, if an expert on the Iron Age is contacted from the museum or history department of a university it is expected he will give a talk to children. Sometimes it could be more useful if he worked with teachers. He could be involved in increasing the teachers' knowledge and in suggesting avenues which would be interesting and useful for the children to explore. Teachers then use their expertise in deciding how these can be tackled by their pupils.

This is a useful approach because it gives teachers the opportunity to tackle areas with which they had little familiarity and to take them to any depth the children are able to pursue. Obviously, able children benefit greatly because they are the ones who will want to probe more deeply and examine more issues. It may be that at some point in the project the outside expert does come into the classroom either to talk on a specific aspect or to elaborate on work already undertaken but it will be in a more closely defined role.

Expertise can also be used by the school in respect of individual exceptional children. Especially in the secondary school children can benefit greatly from having access to people who are already successful in areas that interest them. In some schools individual children have a personal mentor with whom they meet regularly to discuss work. This person often works with the school in establishing a suitable response to the child's needs and offers the child the opportunity to discuss at an appropriate level. Sometimes this can lead to sixth-formers from school making use of higher education laboratories and lectures so enhancing continuity with higher education institutions.

Schools may also make use of individuals from secondary schools or the LEA advisory teams. These too can be used in curriculum planning and, if required, evaluative roles and allow teachers access to a battery of expertise to enhance their own knowledge.

If schools are to provide the best possible curriculum for all their children then all these 'outsiders' have a valuable role to play. Schools need to become more accustomed to asking for help, and to find ways to use visitors effectively. Business is now much more involved in schools and education and its roles in enriching the curriculum could be most useful and lucrative. Many schools already have industry links and business projects but how these can best be used in respect of the more able may not yet be common knowledge. This needs to be explored if bright children are to be encouraged to take a role in industry as advocated by Parliament.

Conclusions

It is evident that curriculum enrichment and extension have implications both within school and outside it. Each of the bodies mentioned in this chapter has a clear and distinct role to play: the LEA to generate and facilitate initiatives and to provide support for individual children; the school to devise effective curriculum approaches and to ensure that these are appropriately implemented and profiled; the class teacher to operate a differentiated approach with particular reference to the needs of the individual; and the parents to be supportive and enthusiastic towards the children and their school.

If all these bodies work in harmony then perhaps the education system will increase its success in turning potential into performance.

Conclusion
Shows - other factors
come into reaching full
potential

Chapter 7

Examples of Good Practice and Personal Experiences

Who to enrich and extend

It is helpful when considering enrichment and extension opportunities to look at the type of children who may take advantage of them. It is tempting to think in terms of a group of highly motivated, articulate individuals whose love of all things appertaining to school will enable them to make the most of the opportunities on offer. In reality, of course, some of the group will be better motivated than others, some will be better team members than others and undoubtedly some will make better use of the opportunities than others because such is the nature of children and learning.

The children described below – Jeremy, Susan, Andrew, Alice, Katie, Roger and Graeme – are all real children. They display the types of characteristics found in children in all classrooms and present the same challenges. The enrichment and extension opportunities which would benefit these children vary from child to child but a close look at the case studies, and responses to them, reveals a pattern of provision which can be incorporated into most classrooms and styles of teaching.

Jeremy is an accomplished talker but loathes written work. He has an encyclopedic mind and soaks up information. He rarely forgets anything he has learnt or read, and so has an extremely wide-ranging general knowledge. He has the ability to amaze his teacher and other adults not only with his general knowledge but also with his grasp of complex adult ideas and issues, eg the parliamentary system. He is seen by other children as a 'little professor', a role which he cultivates. His relationships with other children are reasonable – he is not excluded at playtime, for example – but he treats other children with tolerance rather than seeing himself as one of them.

His handwriting style is spidery and difficult to read and his spelling is erratic. He does not enjoy recording in a written form and tries to avoid it. He does not see a need to record when he can retain so much information in his head. His drawings are at first glance immature but, if given the opportunity, he will explain the complex idea he is seeking to represent.

He loves a challenge and enjoys science and open-ended problem-solving tasks. He will continue to reflect on a problem beyond school requirements and will sometimes present the teacher with an ingenious solution two weeks later. He dislikes doing anything which he sees as pointless and can be very stubborn. Written work falls into the above category as far as Jeremy is concerned!

Comments on Jeremy

In the case of Jeremy any curriculum response will have to take account of the need to develop written skills while at the same time presenting opportunities to undertake really challenging tasks which do not involve him in excessive recording. His development is a delicate balancing act and will without doubt involve considerable effort and tolerance on the part of teachers, parents and the child himself. In writing curriculum enrichment or extension activities for Jeremy's class the teacher would be seeking to create opportunities from which he will benefit.

Susan's parents made her head teacher aware of her exceptional abilities when they came to look round the school. She could read and write fluently and had been tested by an educational psychologist and found to have an IQ of 140+. Susan's parents monitor closely all that she does in school and comment if she undertakes activities which they do not feel are of benefit to her. Susan senses this tension and although at first this made her rather confused and withdrawn, she has now learnt to use it to her advantage. Her manner towards other children has not made her popular as she is inclined to make such comments as, 'Oh! that's easy. I could do that ages ago.'

On a one-to-one basis Susan is a bright, interesting and thoughtful individual and has the potential to be very successful academically but at present does not obtain all that she could from her schooling.

She enjoys tasks which challenge and is confident in her ability to find solutions but quickly loses interest in tasks which involve repetition. She is particularly good with numbers and grasps new concepts quickly. She enjoys investigations but has little time for other children's contributions in this area and always wishes to pursue her own ideas.

Comments on Susan

In Susan's case enrichment and extension activities would provide opportunities for her to work in a meaningful way with other children. Both Susan and her parents would need to understand the purpose of the activities but if such activities were planned and explained to her parents it is likely that a better relationship between home and school would emerge and therefore a better attitude towards school from Susan. This antagonism between the parents of able children and their school is not uncommon and it is worth spending time at the outset in convincing parents of the value of the approach being adopted.

Andrew is a delightful boy to have in class. He is socially well adjusted and exhibits a high degree of aptitude for all tasks set before him. He is always an enthusiastic participant in class activities and has lots of ideas and opinions. He is one of two brothers and comes from an interested, lively family. His parents are very satisfied with his happiness and progress in school and do much to support the school in PTA activities, etc. Out of school time Andrew plays chess, football and is a member of the local Beaver pack. In school he has a large circle of friends and enjoys sport and music.

Academically, he is able to tackle and enjoy all sorts of school activities. He is well motivated, has a good facility with language and reads well. His written work is good and he enjoys meeting new concepts and ideas. He likes to work in a social atmosphere and enjoys tasks which are group based or call for group discussion. Andrew never seems to find any of his school work difficult and very seldom makes errors.

Comments on Andrew

Andrew is 'coasting' at school and while it is good that he is enjoying school and achieving well he does need some opportunities for further challenge. Enrichment tasks in his class should include the chance to explore in depth and to take concepts considerably beyond what might be expected for his age range. He will probably make excellent use of any enrichment or extension activities on offer as he is well motivated and interested.

Alice has proved herself to have well above average ability in maths, reading and written work. She has an exceptional speed of thought, a good memory and a vivid imagination. She is the only child of older professional parents and had little contact with other children before coming to school. She enjoys the company and conversation of adults and is accustomed to long periods of their undivided attention. She finds difficulty in making friends of her own age and is always 'left out' by other children in the class. Playtime and lunchtimes are difficult for her; she loves to sit in a quiet corner and read and always works alone if given the choice. She dislikes having to share her thoughts and ideas with other children and pays little attention to the views and interests of her peers. There are other children in the class who have similar academic potential but none with similar interests.

Alice is rather a serious child by nature and is neat and precise in her work. She likes tasks to have a clear structure and preferably one right answer. She is unsettled by open-ended situations and often chooses the easiest solution in these circumstances. She does not like to be wrong, especially in front of other children, and always seeks to discuss her work, in private, with her teacher.

Comments on Alice
Alice may well feel very threatened by new enrichment and extension activities and so needs a secure classroom environment if she is to tackle them successfully. Enrichment which involves working in a team may provide her with a means of communicating on more equal terms with other children in the class. The fun in finding possible solutions to open-ended questions would need to be stressed and the possibility of failure minimised. Also, Alice needs the chance to work alone and to discuss on a one-to-one basis because this is her favourite form of working.

Katie is a bright, lively child who really enjoys school. She likes to please and is always willing to tidy up the classroom or help her teacher in any way. She has a wide range of interests and a circle of friends with whom to share them. She enjoys playtime and lunchtime and often visits the homes of other children to play after school. She is the older of two sisters and is very supportive to her divorced mother.

In class Katie is always actively involved and makes significant contributions to discussions. She likes to work in a group but is not at all competitive and seldom views her work in terms of the achievement of others. She is inclined to chatter rather more than is strictly necessary but uses this to good effect in group discussions. Katie's work is always neat, tidy, well presented and meets the criteria set by her teacher and Katie does not seem to feel a need to excel. Occasionally, she responds particularly well to a task and produces work of a far higher calibre than is reflected in her normal class work.

Comments on Katie

Katie is typical of many girls in school. We know that girls underperform and this is equally the case for able girls. Peer pressure is important, and therefore the classroom climate must make doing well acceptable and desirable or Katie will not reach her potential. Interesting opportunities of a more unusual nature will often alert teachers to the presence of children like Katie, because it is here that they tend to do well.

Roger came to school with an excellent vocabulary, reading fluently and with an ability to discuss with great maturity. He has a good facility with numbers and a keen appreciation of mathematical concepts. Intellectually, Roger is very able but he finds all written pursuits very difficult and is frustrated by them. He tries to avoid writing wherever possible and in group activities will always encourage other children to do the recording. He dislikes repetitive tasks and often finds that his poor written skills stop him from progressing at school to a level which would meet his intellectual ability. His parents are aware of his mismatch between skills and ability and are keen to help but find Roger unwilling to practise anything written at home.

Roger is confident in his own abilities and enjoys being challenged. He derives great satisfaction from finding interesting solutions to problems and his language work reflects his superb imagination. However, none of this is evident from his written work – he struggles to write and forms letters badly with many reversals. He dislikes any activities which involve drawing or colouring and is beginning to see himself as failing. He is being very difficult and stubborn at home which affects family relationships with his brother and sister and therefore his parents are anxious to find an appropriate response to his needs.

Comments on Roger

Roger is still in the infants. He will need carefully structured enrichment activities if he is to avoid Jeremy's type of problems in later schooling. For him this is a crucial time and enrichment can provide the type of opportunities to challenge his intellectual abilities and so give him a better self-image. When this has been achieved he will be better able to tackle more conventional work. The written work needs to be little and often but with great credit given for even minor success in these areas. Enrichment needs to be stimulating and challenging with the emphasis on thinking rather than recording and credit given for good or innovative ideas.

Graeme has so far found school rather a disappointment. He is exceptionally able, particularly in maths, but this was not obvious as soon as he came to school because he was very quiet and seldom volunteered any information. He learnt to read very quickly and worked his way through the maths tasks without difficulty but did not show much enthusiasm for class activities and seldom responded, except to direct questions, in class discussions.

Graeme's parents visited the school because Graeme was reluctant to attend and expressed the opinion that they felt he was capable of rather more than was expected of him. They had been reluctant to contact the school before since they had little knowledge of the education system, as early school leavers themselves, but were concerned that Graeme saw school as a place to play and home as a place to work. They were worried that he did not enjoy school and that he had failed to make friends.

Recently, Graeme has been informally matched against the National Curriculum levels in maths, science and English and been found, at age 6, to be operating at level 4 in all these areas. He is particularly strong on abstract number concepts and using books for information but is still immature and easily upset. He is starting to make tentative relationships with other children in his class but has little in common with them. His interests are very much those of an average 6-year-old with the intellectual ability of an 11-year-old.

Comments on Graeme

Graeme quite definitely comes in the exceptional child category but is still a 6-year-old in physical and emotional terms. He needs consider-able extension opportunities as well as enrichment. Classroom plan-ning needs to find ways of integrating him and yet also allowing him some chance to work at an appropriate level. Here again the climate in the classroom is all-important. It must be seen as acceptable for him to be special while at the same time allowing him to participate in whole-class activities as much as possible. Tasks which can be done by children of a wide variety of abilities and yet still present challenge to the more able are useful here, for example emergent writing tasks. Similarly, many science tasks can incorporate differing degrees of complexity depending upon the way in which they are presented.

Thankfully, it would be unusual to find all these types of children in one class. Curriculum planning could be something of a nightmare if one needed to plan for such diverse needs, but elements of these needs are found in all classes and that is precisely why enrichment and extension need to be flexible both in terms of content and process. From looking at these children it becomes obvious that work in teams and groups has a role in enrichment as does the open-ended problem-solving approach, but variety of approach is the key because the wider the variety of types of opportunity the greater the number of children likely to take advantage of the challenge.

Some examples of good practice

Included here are some examples of enrichment and extension in practice. The contributions are from colleagues from both primary and secondary schools and reflect a variety of practice and approaches. Some are concerned with establishing provision in school and describe how they come to look at enrichment and extension as a method of providing for their able children, what they did and initial reactions. Others reflect a more established pattern of provision where continued development has led to reflection and subsequent adjustment in approach and provision. We are very grateful to these colleagues for taking time out of their busy schedules to write these reports for there is no substitute for first-hand experience and practice.

1. VALLEY ROAD PRIMARY SCHOOL – GETTING STARTED
In this report the staff of Valley Road Primary School explain their reasons for getting started and how they approached the task. Valley Road is a small primary school and the head and staff have worked closely to establish a co-ordinated response. Like most primary schools, Valley Road has a policy on provision for less able children. This deals with matters such as teaching strategies, grouping organisation and resources.

We now felt that we should address the needs of the more able with the same positive spirit. As a result of this decision, contact was made with the General Adviser for the Special Needs of More Able Children.

Initially, we had a meeting with Mike Deans, the Adviser, and Deborah Eyre, the Advisory Teacher. They visited the school and later joined a staff meeting where we discussed some of the issues involved in formulating a policy. For example, what constitutes ability? How to recognise it, what to do about it, etc. It was agreed that Deborah would return with a selection of resources as it was felt that this was a key factor in helping to extend the more able.

We spent several staff meetings clarifying the issues and agreeing some key statements of policy which we could later take to the governors. As a result of these meetings we formulated the following principles:

- There should be a whole-staff approach to able children.

- Valley Road should provide a curriculum of opportunity.
- Staff would look at teaching strategies which would help meet the needs of the more able.
- Resources would be sought and made to support the curriculum.
- The LEA's help would be encouraged.
- The identification of the able would be wide enough to cover a large number of children.

It should be said in this context that the staff felt much more comfortable with the term 'more able' than with the label 'gifted' with all its connotations of precocious talent.

At the next meeting, we decided that our whole-school approach would take the form of a whole-school topic, which would offer opportunities for challenging children, provide enrichment and extension activities and would be more skills based than before.

We would use the topic to try out different teaching strategies particularly the devising and provision of open-ended tasks which would stretch the children and encourage creativity. Children who had finished initial tasks would be offered extension/enrichment tasks, not more practice of what they had just completed.

We chose the topic 'Communications' because we felt it was extensive enough to provide opportunities for all the strategies we had discussed.

At further meetings there were brainstorming sessions and webs were produced to show the cross-curricular links. Resources were ordered and contact was made with British Telecom, ITV, BBC and the local radio and newspaper. The topic lasted for the whole of the spring term and at the end of the term we had a meeting to evaluate what we had achieved.

At the evaluation meeting focus was initially on the environmental aspects of the topic, eg the term was too short, the topic was too wide. We came to understand that if you choose a whole-school topic that is too wide it ceases to be one topic and becomes a set of separate topics. That said, we set about evaluting the topic in the context of stretching the more able.

- Genuine excitement had been generated in the school by virtue of the fact that everyone was studying the same topic.
- The result of all staff input in the planning stages was a very rich pot of ideas. We were able to use the various organisational strengths of the team, eg completer-finisher, resource investigator, etc. The result was a well-implemented topic with everyone making a good contribution.
- The children were being stretched by the provision of a learning environment which depended more on new age strategies than a new age topic.

It was decided to repeat the experiment in the autumn term of 1989 but to spend the summer term consolidating the strategies and resources that had been successful in our class topics.

Towards the end of the summer term, 1989, we had a planning meeting for the coming term with Deborah Eyre. The new members of staff were invited and we successfully planned our topic, 'Journeys'.

This time the topic was a manageable size and could be followed across the age ranges. It gave plenty of scope for the challenging skills of graph work and for problem-solving with timetables, tidetables and currency exchange tables. It also brought in foreign languages and we were interested to see how quickly children would pick up a working vocabulary when motivated.

We have used the whole-school topic to help us stretch our more able. The results so far have been encouraging. Motivation is good in both staff and children. Parents are involved; the local community is involved. There is a striving towards excellence and the children have been set goals, coached in the skills necessary to achieve the goals and then enabled to get on and do it.

Finally, I would make the following points:

- What we have done so far is to provide a curriculum of opportunity where ability can flourish.
- We have focused so far on thinking skills and, to a large extent, practical skills.
- We have resourced and supported the project with loans from the Curriculum Enrichment Centre and by selective purchase and provision of suitable materials.

We have made a start.

Ann Wilson, Valley Road School, Henley

2. COPING WITH THE MORE ABLE – DIDCOT GIRLS SCHOOL

In this report Didcot Girls School, like Valley Road, made a conscious staff decision to look at its opportunities for the more able. Here, too, this was a natural extension of looking at special needs for the less able and a whole-staff approach was developed.

We are a semi-rural, 11–18, all-girl comprehensive school. Over recent years our learning support department has responded to the terms of the 1981 Education Act in such a way as to embrace all areas of special needs, including the more able. This latter area is new and in its earliest stages of implementation.

Development

1987. Appointment of a new head teacher rekindled earlier interest in the needs of more able pupils.

1987. Autumn term – questionnaire to all staff to find out current provision for bright pupils and attitudes to singling them out.

1988. Spring term – head of learning support on full-time secondment to investigate various models of more able provision and to propose one for our school.

1988. Baker Day – whole-staff focus on more able organised by head of learning support and a deputy head, covering the following aspects:

- introductory talk by head and by Ron Arnold
- cross-curricular group discussion
- subject department discussion groups
- 2 and 3 to devise short- and long-term strategies for extending/enriching the education of the more able.

Present practice
(a) Learning support team has gone over to support teaching in mixed ability classes in maths, science and English in years 1 and 2 (withdrawal is retained for 'special' cases throughout the school).
(b) Education extra is run by a deputy head.
(c) List of characteristics of more able handed out to all staff. In two weeks' time all first years will be tested in verbal, quantitive and non-verbal skills. This way we hope to identify our more able.
(d) Monitoring of strategies devised by subject departments to take place immediately after half-term.
(e) One teacher has been awarded an extra allowance for one term to look into resources for the more able.
(f) Examples of ideas thought up by the subject departments are not available.

I am optimistic for the future!

Sylvia Jordan, Didcot Girls School

3. IT STARTED BY ACCIDENT – FARINGDON SCHOOL
As its title suggests this third report started in a different way from the previous two! Faringdon School, a comprehensive in a market town, developed its interest through the enthusiasm of its deputy head. The resulting approach was different but demonstrates well the flexibility of enrichment and extension as a method of provision.

(a) It started by accident. Some INSET days are tedious, others change your life. Listening to David George at Nene College, Northampton opened up a whole new way of thought to me and made me realise how inadequate it was simply to provide a 'top set' as a school response to the more able child.
(b) I joined the school to the National Association for Curriculum Enrichment, of which David George is the president, read their leaflets and attended their annual conference. Dr George came very willingly to Faringdon to speak to the staff in an attempt to raise awareness.
(c) One or two little things started to happen. I ran a lunchtime Spanish group in two half hours a week for about ten months in an attempt to catch the last of the O levels. It was a mixed group of able third years and interested lower sixth-formers. I did not exclude anyone from

opting in from my top set. Consequently some did (whom I would not have advised), some did not (who could have coped). In the event, the grades were A, B, 2 × C, 2 × D and 3 × U. Inconclusive – but a start and some highly motivated children, one of whom has gone on to gain an A in GCSE Latin.

(d) While our pupils are required to find their own work experience at the end of their fourth year, the head of science has been able to make the most of some superb placements locally in scientific and electronic establishments. This has led to the pupils doing extended work experience in these places and being given specific projects to do by the companies. In some cases, the pupil has designed or created something which has been adopted by the company. In one case, having not followed the course at school, a boy entered for A level computer studies at the last minute (in the fifth form) and got a grade C, as well as nine GCSE passes.

(e) An electronics club started at lunchtime. A parent provides regular and significant input to this. The attendance has revealed certain youngsters whom one could describe as 'talented' rather than 'more able'. We have been surprised at the skill shown by some of our pupils in this area which has not come out in other sections of the curriculum.

(f) A pupil has come to light in our first year who is years ahead in French – he is functioning at good fourth-year standard. We have therefore taken the plunge and decided to teach him individually using a variety of materials: books, videos, cassettes and computer programs. A pupil of this type raises all sorts of curriculum questions about the phrase in everyone's brochure which says 'we value the education of each child equally'.

(g) In response to my circular (see note (i) below) colleagues have approached me offering to run Latin as an interest/exam course and there is talk of reintroducing a competitive chess club.

(h) A colleague is working with a pupil deemed to be 'on strike' by his primary school who, according to tests, appears to have a very high IQ. At the moment, on an individual basis, computer programs – both doing and writing – are being put in his way with good results.

(i) Now that I have passed on the overall responsibility for special needs in the school to a fellow deputy head, I am able to devote more time to finding a school attitude to this phenomenon. I have now circulated the staff with some ideas for purchasing some self-support and self-marking materials, for contacting parents and for making more use of lunch-times and extension materials. We have in existence a cross-curriculum group, the Special Needs Curriculum Group, where this can be debated.

Thus we have arrived at take-off point!

Richard Arrowsmith, Faringdon School

4. HOLYPORT CE PRIMARY SCHOOL

This school has a head teacher with a long-standing interest in children with potential. Provision here has grown through a variety of approaches, each one showing the school's developing understanding of the children and issues involved. The emphasis has moved from dealing with individual children to high quality provision for all children – enrichment and extension.

I am the head teacher of a Group 5 Church of England primary school. The school is situated in a large village with a catchment area of middle class, commuterland parents with above average ability children.

My interest in gifted children goes back to 1971 when I attended a weekend course, at our local Teacher's Centre, tutored by Ralph Callow, but it was not until my appointment to my second headship in April 1979 that I had the opportunity to put my thoughts and ideas into practice.

I was able to appoint a Scale 2 postholder with responsibility for curriculum extension for the able child. Like most jobs in the primary school, Deborah had a full-time teaching commitment and worked mainly in an advisory capacity. During the spring and summer of 1980 she and I attended a Regional DES course on able children at Reading University, and this gave us the basis to start work at Holyport. In staff meetings during those two terms we developed strategies for identifying able children.

- The staff identified the children in their own teams whom they considered able and talented.
- The results from NFER tests of maths, English and verbal reasonings were looked at. These tests are school-administered every year, three weeks into the autumn term. I feel that we get a truer picture of a child's ability early in the autumn term than in June/July.
- Any child who had a wide discrepancy in her test results or who appeared on the staff list but not on the test list or vice versa had a non-verbal test.
- In a small number of cases where we were still not sure we discussed the child with parents.
- Finally, in one or two cases we asked the educational psychologist for an option.

Using the above we then identified a group of junior-aged children who were talented in the fields of maths and language and these were withdrawn once a week for extension work. This system worked very well for 18 months although it highlighted a number of advantages and disadvantages. The staff's awareness of children's varying abilities had been heightened and they were beginning to question why we were covering only one facet of the above child categories, mainly high intellect, and then only in maths and English. In their search for 'gold they had found silver' and they now wanted to develop a school policy that would provide for a wide range of gifts and talents. It was decided to tackle this problem in two ways.

Firstly, we extended the resources in the school. This meant allocating money on a regular basis to purchase books, games, workcards, etc that could be used as extension material. There was, and still is, very little published under this specific heading and therefore we had to look at existing publications and suggest alternative ways of using them. This resource bank is now very large and covers all areas of the curriculum. It still has an annual budget in the same way as maths, art or music. It is centralised in the entrance hall of the school and all children are encouraged to use it.

Secondly, we decided to set up an activities afternoon each week. The idea was to provide approximately 20 different activities on a termly basis and cover as many interesting experiences as possible, asking the parents if they could offer a talent or hobby that they were prepared to share with the children. We also contacted local advisers: the church groups, the Darby and Joan, in fact anyone whom we felt could help us! The response was fantastic and for two years we ran an enormous range of experiences for the children – from the usual school subjects of maths and science, to hobbies such as macramé, model-making and cookery, to specialist subjects like astronomy, campanology, architecture and church history.

The postholder for the above child, now a Scale 3, had responsibility for organising the afternoons. Julie arranged that all non-teachers had groups of eight children while teachers had varying groups according to their activity. Every square inch of the school came into use and children explored the delights of music-making or scientific experiments or gardening. Initially, children were allowed to choose which activity they joined for the team. As the scheme progressed so children were encouraged to join certain activities to give them a chance to explore their latent talents, often with surprising results.

After two years it was time to reassess the situation. Parents were beginning to help only with the activities afternoons, not with individual children or groups during the rest of the week. Other volunteer help was 'drying up' and the momentum to keep the afternoons interesting and stimulating was becoming more and more difficult.

We were now on to our third postholder. Judith was an infant specialist, and that brought fresh impetus to the staff. It was felt that the children's curriculum development should be catered for within the classroom situation. Each year group works as a team of approximately 60 children with two staff. Each team chooses a termly topic that is brainstormed to include as many aspects of the curriculum as possible. Flow diagrams are prepared to show the development of the topic and assignments written for the different levels of ability. Though the children are initially directed to the assignment suitable for their needs, this does not preclude any child from tackling different levels, often with interesting results.

The problems of writing assignments are then open-ended and challenging. It is not easy; in fact, some staff find it very difficult. To help staff, a number of meetings were spent looking at open-ended questioning and the way to write interesting tasks. These sessions threw up the need to look in depth at study skills. Each team wrote a list of the skills they would expect to teach in a year and these were collected by all staff into a study skills document for 5 to 11-year-olds.

In the meanwhile we had, as a staff, completed writing our policy statements on the curriculum for all the major areas and felt it was time to commit to paper our policy on the able child. As usual a term's staff meetings were devoted to discussion and a paper was eventually produced and submitted to the governors.

[See Figure 6.1 on page 86 for details of the policy document.]

The fourth current postholder is a member of the junior department and has, for 18 months, had a monitoring role. We continue to add to our resources on a regular basis but with the advent of the Education Reform Act, and in particular the National Curriculum, we will need to ensure that the differentiated curriculum continues to be addressed. For after all, in the words of Cardinal Newman, 'to live is to change and to be perfect is to have changed often'.

Johanna Raffan, Holyport CE Primary School

5. SOME ISSUES CONCERNED WITH ESTABLISHING A PROGRAMME FOR MORE ABLE CHILDREN AT HENRY BOX SCHOOL

This final report concerns a comprehensive school with established provision for the more able. Here development through the learning support unit has created opportunities to provide enrichment and extension on a number of different levels. Effective provision does not happen overnight and even with eight years' experience Henry Box School is still learning!

As a permanent member of the learning support department (LSD) of this 1000-strong comprehensive school in rural Oxfordshire, I was given the brief, three years ago, to examine the provision for 'more able' pupils in mixed ability entry forms. The phrase 'more able' was chosen in preference to 'gifted' as the latter concept appeared to be rather narrow and difficult to define. The term also seemed less 'elitist' and I was keen to avoid any immediate, negative responses from colleagues when embarking on this project, although Denton and Postlethwaite, during their research into teachers' attitudes in Oxfordshire had found that

'teachers are becoming increasingly interested in the importance of trying to meet the individual pupil's particular educational needs wherever that pupil lies on the spectrum of abilities.'

(Denton and Postlethwaite, 1982)

The whole school ethos is that all pupils should be given every educational opportunity to develop their potential and that each subject department has the responsibility for the progress of pupils within that subject area. The learning support department operates a flexible timetable with four full-time, professional staff and one full-time classroom assistant, using team-teaching and individual or group withdrawal methods.

Within this context I examined the contribution that could be made by the learning support department to the general progress of pupils who were consistently achieving or who were considered 'able' pupils but who were thought to be underachieving. I drew several observations and suggestions together in a discussion document which was distributed to all members of the teaching staff.

This proved an important step in raising the awareness of colleagues. It became increasingly important when attempting to influence school policy and practice that colleagues were involved in the process of change at every stage. The next stage in the process of consultation which led to the formation of a whole-school policy for the provision for more able pupils was a full staff meeting at which Keith Postlethwaite, who was then at the department of education at the University of Oxford, spoke about his work with more able pupils in the areas of maths, science and French. I spoke briefly at the same meeting about the issues which were raised in the discussion paper. This was followed up some weeks later by a questionnaire arising from the paper which was issued to departments for discussion during directed time. The results of the questionnaires led to a final document which was considered by senior staff and a full meeting of governors before becoming accepted as school policy.

Throughout these procedures I felt it was necessary to clarify the LSD ethos that 'all children have specific and individual needs whatever their ability'. The more able pupils are a group of children whose special educational needs were implicitly recognised in the Warnock Report (1978) and the subsequent Education Act of 1981. The LSD considers that work with this group of children is one aspect of the wider task of providing for the whole range of special educational needs. Elitism proved not to be an issue in our school and neither was it necessary to justify the LSD's involvement in the project since departmental liaison is efficient; each department has a representative responsible for the children with special educational needs and there are regular cross-departmental 'links' meetings with the LSD.

Although the approach to the teaching of the more able varied through the school, the LSD fulfilled a central role by acting as an agency for collecting and storing test data on all pupils together with information about available teaching resources. Data is now held on all pupils from the first year upwards. The department initiated a scheme for feeder primary schools to administer tests to future Henry Box pupils (including the Junior Edinburgh reading test), the results of which form the first layer of data. Added to these results are the NFER non-verbal test, the Edinburgh reading test and Blackwell's spelling test, all of which are administered by the learning support department within the school. These results can be correlated with other information such as the number of top sets a pupil has been placed in. The information is updated after full reports have been issued to parents and feedback obtained from parents' evenings. A system of referral forms (which each member of staff can fill in and return to the department at any stage pointing out excellent achievement or concern about a previously well-motivated or achieving pupil) aids the updating procedure. Checklists are used by staff at all levels of assessment.

The issues involved in producing and running programmes for the more able were much more complex. It was agreed from the start that the LSD could not and should not run the exercise in isolation. The main thrust of education takes place in the mainstream during the school day and many departments were already providing for their more able students within the existing curriculum framework. It was accepted that most teachers had their own methods for identifying their most able students and providing them with challenging assignments. The completed departmental questionnaires highlighted where the LSD could facilitate the implementation of programmes by providing resources, withdrawing or monitoring specific children. In some cases it became expedient for LSD staff to supervise a larger teaching group while the specialist teacher withdrew selected children to carry out extension work. The same system applied in the production of resources. Time may be made available for departments to work on enrichment materials during allocated 'Baker Days'.

Several departments have taken advantage of 'Education Extra' funding to bring in experts to work with specific pupils during the school day. The art department have had a sculptor and printer in residence. The funding is administered by the head of the LSD.

In addition to the mainstream initiative, extra-curricular, day-release and long-term residential courses were instigated and run by the LSD. They operate on an opt-in policy and are funded by parental contribution. Specific pupils are targeted but other pupils wishing to take part are not excluded. Pupils are excused from normal lessons on the understanding that classwork and homework will be completed in the pupils' own time. Support from the other members of the teaching staff is essential if such programmes are to become a regular part of the curriculum. It is particularly difficult to evalute such activities. A pupil profile record sheet has been devised which complies with the OCEA (Oxfordshire Certificate of Educational Achievement) guidelines and which student and teacher complete together, but more efficient methods of appraisal are still being sought.

Providing for the educational needs of any pupil is a complicated process since one needs to consider a large number of permutations of contributors to the whole process. A whole-school policy for Henry Box was essential if provision for more able pupils was to be organised, continuous and developmental. The policy is still being developed and adapted to meet the demands of other educational initiatives but it has provided a foundation upon which to build provision for many students.

Sue McMillan, Henry Box School, Witney

Comments
These reports cover a wide variety of approaches and practice but certain facts emerge in terms of establishing effective provision:

- A school must see a need.
- One member of staff must take on responsibility for co-ordinating provision although the day-to-day provision remains every teacher's concern.
- Senior management within the school must support and encourage the provision if all colleagues in the school are to be persuaded to participate.
- The school must monitor and discuss the effectiveness of its approaches.
- Provision must suit the school and its existing organisation.

Writing enrichment materials

There is no correct way to write enrichment materials. They are an extension to a teacher's normal planning and therefore will be written in whatever format is used by that teacher in the classroom. However, there are some principles and guidelines which can usefully be considered.

1. AIMS AND OBJECTIVES

It is important to be quite clear about what one hopes to achieve with the materials. There are likely to be overall objectives for the topic or project and, in addition, more sharply focused objectives for each task.

For example, the overall aim in Townscapes (LDA, 1988) is to 'provide stimulating and challenging materials for the 9–13 age range' and to develop certain listed skills:

- 'Collating and evaluating information.
- Decision-making.
- Developing classification skills.
- The ability to draw conclusions and make judgments.
- Problem-solving.
- Developing social and intellectual skills.
- Understanding and solving technological problems.
- Encouraging creativity.'

The project also has separate objectives for each of its 12 activities and an understanding of the skills which it seeks to foster.

2. HOW TO START

Once again this will be dependent to some extent on the teacher's usual method of working but a useful starting point is through brainstorming the idea or subject, preferably with colleagues, and then creating a *spider chart* of ideas. It is important to make the chart as full as possible

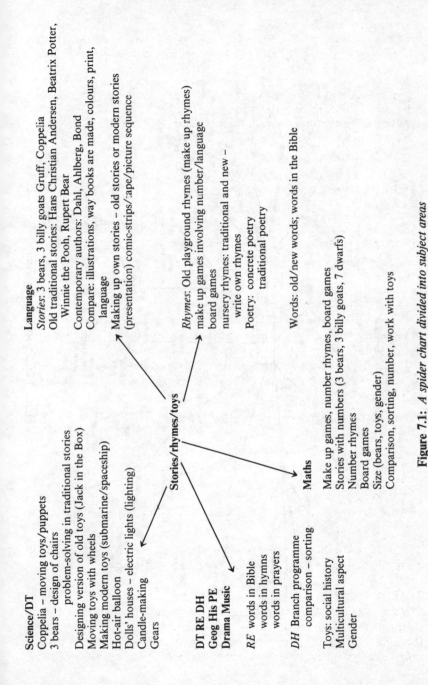

Language

Stories: 3 bears, 3 billy goats Gruff, Coppelia
Old traditional stories: Hans Christian Andersen, Beatrix Potter, Winnie the Pooh, Rupert Bear
Contemporary authors: Dahl, Ahlberg, Bond
Compare: illustrations, way books are made, colours, print, language
Making up own stories – old stories or modern stories
(presentation) comic-strips/tape/picture sequence

Rhymes: Old playground rhymes (make up rhymes)
make up games involving number/language
board games
nursery rhymes: traditional and new – write own rhymes
Poetry: concrete poetry
traditional poetry

Words: old/new words; words in the Bible

Maths

Make up games, number rhymes, board games
Stories with numbers (3 bears, 3 billy goats, 7 dwarfs)
Number rhymes
Board games
Size (bears, toys, gender)
Comparison, sorting, number, work with toys

Stories/rhymes/toys

Science/DT

Coppelia – moving toys/puppets
3 bears – design of chairs
problem-solving in traditional stories
Designing version of old toys (Jack in the Box)
Moving toys with wheels
Making modern toys (submarine/spaceship)
Hot-air balloon
Dolls' houses – electric lights (lighting)
Candle-making
Gears

**DT RE DH
Geog His PE
Drama Music**

RE words in Bible
words in hymns
words in prayers

DH Branch programme
comparison – sorting

Toys: social history
Multicultural aspect
Gender

Figure 7.1: *A spider chart divided into subject areas*

115

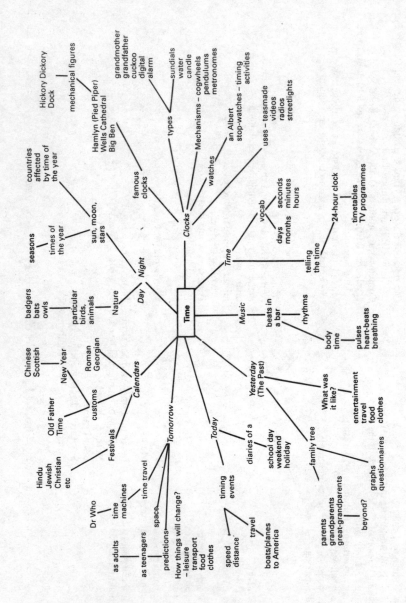

Figure 7.2: *Spider chart on 'Time'*

without considering how an idea can be incorporated. This is because at the later stage of devising tasks it is helpful to have the maximum variety of ideas which can be moulded into a task rather than deciding on an objective or skill and being unable to find a task to match it. When writing spider charts many teachers subdivide their ideas into subject areas (see Figure 7.1). While at first glance this may seem attractive, many ideas are cross-curricular or do not immediately fall into any curriculum area. Therefore, a spider chart based on themes (see Figure 7.2) may well provide a wider range of opportunities.

In the chart on Time (Figure 7.2) the group have identified eight major themes and subdivided these. The chart is a record of random thoughts and ideas but these are so plentiful that any one of the sections could be a topic on its own. There are a wide variety of ideas so it would be easy to devise tasks which will appeal to widely differing children. A chart of this type lends itself to National Curriculum attainment levels. It is just as easy to slot ATs into this type of chart as into the more conventional one.

3. WRITING THE TASKS

Each task should take account of content and process as well as being well matched to the children who will undertake it. Examples of good tasks are to be found in many of the materials listed in Chapter 9. For example, in 'The Motorway Project Pack' (LDA LD400), task 3 (see Figure 7.3) refers to the building of a motorway. Children are asked to

---

Figure 7.3: *The Motorway Project Pack*

Activity Card 3

Ashwell Manor and Home Farm

It is generally agreed that there is a need to build a motorway in the area, bypassing the nearby town. There is, however, a conflict of interest (see *Information Sheet 4*).

With a partner, take one of the estates each and prepare a report explaining which line you prefer. Say why your estate should be maintained perhaps to the detriment of your neighbour's.

When you have both prepared your reports, arrange with your teacher to hold a court inquiry at which you can present the case to the rest of your class, who will act as decision-makers.

Two lines along which the motorway might pass have been proposed. For convenience these lines will be referred to as Plan A and Plan B.

PLAN A
- This would sever 145 acres of the Ashwell Estate.
- This would take 13–16 acres from Home Farm.
- The view from Ashwell Manor would be destroyed as the road would be 3 metres high. Landscaping would be necessary as Little Thrift Wood would be damaged and another wood destroyed.
- An agricultural crossing at Thrift Lane would cost an extra £40,000.
- The noise effect on the Ashwell Estate would be greater.

PLAN B
- This would sever 98 acres of the Ashwell Estate.
- This would take 18–30 acres from Home Farm.
- The two main woodlands would be left, thereby screening Ashwell House.
- Less compensation would be required by Ashwell Manor with the smaller severance. There would be a saving of £104,000 as the line is shorter.
- The noise on Home Farm would be greater.

Information Sheet 4

Ashwell Manor

The Broadhurst family have lived at Ashwell Manor for over 300 years. The present Mr Broadhurst is an elderly gentleman having no immediate family to succeed him. On his death the estate will pass to a distant cousin who at present works on the oil rigs in the North Sea.

Ashwell Manor, a thriving arable farm extending some 675 acres, is intensively farmed as a single unit. Although no livestock movements are at present involved, this could be a possibility for the future. It would be difficult to administer the estate if it were split, for example for driving the combine harvester or transferring stock.

The house was originally built in 1466, and is one of the most complete manor houses of the fifteenth century still remaining. it is described by Nicholas Pevsner as 'The most refined and most sophisticated timber frame mansion in England.' It is famous for its contemporary heraldic glass.

There are two main woods on the estate contributing to the historic setting, the biggest being Little Thrift Wood, which has become an important conservation area because of the rare birds which have established a nesting site there.

The Ashwell land is covered by a covenant with the National Trust, although part of the estate has been sold and developed with private housing. There was a fear it might have been under a compulsory purchase order for council housing. Although this housing is near the Manor to the north, it is separated by a high wall.

What gives the house more character, however, is the prospect to the south of parkland, largely cultivated, with occasional tree clumps and framed in the distance by Little Thrift Wood and the wood north-east of it, with no foreign intrusion into the landscape. While the view from the downstairs windows of the house is masked by yew trees, that from an upstairs window is clear and the landscape already described is in full view.

The covenant is to protect the land, house and gardens from undesirable alteration, although the estate is not open to the public.

Home Farm

Mr Williams is a specialist dairy farmer, on 97 acres. He owns 52 acres, including 1.5 acres for house and buildings. He leases a further 45 acres. He wishes to preserve as much of his holding as possible.

At present his farm is an efficient dairy unit producing high quality milk. He holds a pedigree stock of 95 head of cattle, which will shortly be increased to 110, with 55 milkers. This stock has a planned output of 135 gallons per day, to be achieved by fertility improvement of the land and the use of modern buildings, under the advice of, and with grants from, the Ministry of Agriculture. Mr Williams, his wife and son depend for their living on the farm. He is highly thought of by the Ministry and he has been selected for visits by foreign delegations to inspect his layout and methods.

Mr Williams bought the farm seven years ago, although the Development Plan of 1953 had mentioned the proposed line of a motorway. The farmstead and part of the land is contained within a conservation area which includes several old houses centred around the local village green. Certain parts of the farm are of historic interest, notably the medieval tithe barn.

There is the possibility of buying other land in the vicinity, as he requires a minimum woking acreage of 85 acres. However, a split site would create many difficulties in the movement of cattle.

read the information and then use it to present a report to the rest of the class. Here the task accomplishes a number of different functions:

- it is interesting and relevant and so is likely to appeal to children
- the children have not only to read and understand quite complex text but also to demonstrate their understanding by reusing the information in a different form
- the child presents the task to the class, so allowing for some drama and role-playing
- presentation does not rely on a written report but could make use of a wide variety of high-tec equipment.

In much the same way the task 'Minibeasts Safari Guide' provides interest, challenge and some opportunities for imagination and laterial thinking:

Devise a guide to the minibeasts in the wildlife area. Things to think about:

- Will you need to look at other guidebooks?
- Who will use the guide?
- Will the guide be written or taped?
- Will you need a map, guide-posts, etc?
- Should you run a pilot scheme to test effectiveness?

Tasks do not have to be lengthy in description: 'Design chairs for the three bears – daddy bear, mummy bear and baby bear' has all the same elements of interest, challenge, open-ended opportunity but within design/technology (DT)

'List as many ways as you can to make the answer 10.' The same elements occur again but this time in simple maths. It is not so much the content which is important, so long as it is suitable, but the way in which it is handled. None of the above examples comes from the National Curriculum documents but they all allow children to achieve at high levels on the attainment targets if they are able.

Bruner (1966) says that problem-solving must:

'have exploration through activation, motivation and direction. Cut-and-dried tasks have too little exploration. Ones that are too uncertain may arouse confusion and anxiety with the effect of reducing exploration'.

This is equally relevant to writing tasks for enrichment and extension.

4. TASK CHECKLIST
The following checklist may prove useful when writing a task:

- What are its aims?
- Does the task have the right degree of open-endedness?
- Does it have a right answer or can a range of answers be justified?
- How is information to be recorded – written, tape, DT, OHP, etc?
- Is there an opportunity to reframe what has been learnt?
- Can role-play be included?
- Does it involve difficult material? If so, are the goals clearly defined?
- Have you phased it carefully, especially if the type of task is unfamiliar?
- Volume. Is it too long to retain interest or so short children can't get going?

- Children like humour, choice, puzzles, codes and clues.

Recording outcomes

A final note in this chapter concerns recording the outcomes of enrichment and extension. Much emphasis is, at present, placed upon results and outcomes and yet the skills which enrichment and extension seek to foster, ie those of thinking and related skills, are difficult to record. Few profiles or records of achievement record that a child has consistently innovative ideas in design/technology or that a child exhibits leadership skills in group activities. If enrichment and extension are to be valued by parents and colleagues it is important to incorporate recognition of the wider body of skills which this approach seeks to foster.

Chapter 8
Helpful Organisations

Many of the following organisations, associations and societies have education sections or departments or they produce curriculum materials and other publications of value to the teacher.

General

Association for the Study of the Curriculum
Education Offices
Chapel Street
Salford M3 5LT

European Association of Teachers
20 Brookfield
Highgate West Hill
London N6 6AS

NACE (National Association for Curriculum Enrichment and Extension)
Moulton Park
Northampton NN2 7AL
Secretary Mr M Turner at
Ohmagen
Nettleton Road
Burton
Chippenham
Wilts SN14 7LR

Annual conference, newsletter, many curriculum materials (see Chapter 9).

NAGC (National Association for Gifted Children)
Now sharing accommodation with NACE at Nene College. Consultancy work for gifted children, holiday courses, national and regional meetings, Saturday clubs, some publications.

Questors – The Potential Trust
Shepherds Close
Kingston Stert
nr Chinnor
Oxon OX9 4NL
Organises holiday courses, produces news-sheet and 'Quest-Ions' problem/project material.

Art

Design Council
28 Haymarket
London SW1Y 4SU

National Society for Education in Art and Design
7a High Street
Corsham
Wilts SN13 0ES

Society for Education Through Art
Bath Academy of Art
Corsham
Wilts

Classics

Classical Association
University College
PO Box 78
Cardiff CF1 1XL

Joint Association of Classical Teachers
31–34 Gordon Square
London WC1H 0PY

Society for Promotion of Hellenic Studies and Society for Promotion of Roman Studies
31–34 Gordon Square
WC1H 0PY

English and drama

The English Association
The Vicarage
Priory Gardens
Bedford Park
London W4 1TT

English Speaking Union
Dartmouth House
37 Charles Street
London W1X 8AB

National Association for Drama in Education and Children's Theatre
91 Old Orchard Road
Eastbourne
East Sussex BN21 1DD

National Association for Teaching of English
Birley School Annexe
Fox Lane Site
Frecheville
Sheffield S12 4WY

National Poetry Centre
24 Earls Court Square
London SW5 9DE

Film and visual aids

British Film Institute
21 Stephen Street
London W1P 1PL

Educational Foundation for Visual Aids
PO Box 566
25 High Street
Maidenhead SL6 1NP

Welsh Office Film Unit
Crown Buildings
Cathays Park
Cardiff CF1 3NQ

HE (Home Economics)

Institute of Home Economics Ltd
71–91 Aldwych
London WC2B 4HN

History, geography and social science

Association for Teaching of Social Sciences
Pineleigh
Silverdale Road
Arnside
Carnforth
Lancs

Geographical Association
343 Fulwood Road
Sheffield S10 3BP

Industrial Society
48 Bryanston Square
London W1

National Trust
36 Queen Anne's Gate
London SW1H 9AS

Royal Geographical Society
1 Kensington Gore
London SW7 2AR

Mathematics

Association of Teachers of Mathematics
7 Shaftesbury Street
Derby DE3 8YB

Institute of Mathematics and its Applications
Maitlands House
Warrior Square
Southend on Sea
Essex SS1 2JY

Mathematics Association
259 London Road
Leicester LE2 3BE

Modern languages

Association of Teachers of German
Regents College
Regents Park
London NW1 4NS

Association of Teachers of Italian
St Paul's School
London SW13 9JT

Association of Teachers of Russian
7 Cherry Tree Court
Sheffield S1 9AP

Association of Teachers of Spanish and Portuguese
32 Gledhow Lane
Leeds LS8 1SA

British Association for Language Teaching
67 Glenmoor Park Road
Skelly
Swansea SA2 0QE

Modern Language Association
Regents College
Regents Park
London NW1 4NS

Museums

Group for Education in Museums
Bucks County Museum
Aylesbury
Bucks HP20 2QP

Museums Association
34 Bloomsbury Way
London WC1A 2SF

Music

English Folk Dance and Song Society
Cecil Sharp House
2 Regents Park Road
London NW1 7AY

Music Advisers National Association
Avon House North
St James Barton
Bristol BS99 7EB

Music Masters and Mistresses Association
White Cottage
Church Road
Steep
Petersfield
Hants

Youth and Music
78 Neal Street
Covent Garden
London WC2H 9PA

Puppets

Puppet Centre Trust
Battersea Arts Centre
Lavender Hill
London SW11 5TJ

RE (Religious Education)

National Society for Promoting RE
Church House
Deers Yard
London SW1P 3NZ

Radices (Religious Drama Society of GB)
Christchurch and Upton Chapel
Kensington Road
London SE1 7QP

Religious Education Council
2 Romeland Hill
St Albans
Herts AL3 4ET

Scripture Union in Schools
130 City Road
London EC1V 2NJ

Science and technology

Association for Science Education
College Lane
Hatfield
Herts AL10 9AA

Botanical Society of the British Isles
Department of Botany
British Museum for Natural History
Cromwell Road
London SW7 5BD

Earth Science Teachers Association
20 Petworth Close
Middleton
Manchester M24 1QH

Educational Field Studies
60 Southlea Road
Havant
Hants PO9 2QJ

Field Studies Council
Preston Montford
Montford Bridge
Shrewsbury SY4 1HW

Geologists Association
Burlington House
Piccadilly
London W1V 0JU

Institute of Biology
20 Queensbury Place
London SW7 2DS

Institute of Physics
47 Belgrave Square
London SW1X 9QX

**National Association for
Environmental Education**
West Midlands College of
Further Education
Walsall WS1 3RD

Nuffield Foundation
Nuffield Lodge
Regents Park
London NW1 4RS

Royal Meteorological Society
James Glaisher House
Grenville Place
Bracknell
Berks RG12 1BX

**RSPB and Young Ornithologists
Club**
The Lodge
Sandy
Beds SG19 2DI

Technology

**National Council for Educational
Technology**
3 Devonshire Street
London W1N 3BA

**National Design and Technology
Foundation**
45 Bournemouth Road
Chandlers Ford
Hants SO5 3DJ

Primary Technology Project
Pendower Hall
West Road
Newcastle-on-Tyne NE15 6PP

**Society for the Advancement of
Games and Simulation in
Education and Training**
Centre for External Studies
University of Technology
Loughborough
Leicester LE11 3TU

**Standing Conference on School
Science and Technology**
1 Birdcage Walk
London SW1H 9JJ

**Trent International Centre for
School Technology**
Trent Polytechnic
Burton Street
Nottingham NG1 4BU

Chapter 9

What Exists Already

With all the changes and extra tasks imposed on teachers today there
is no time to be wasted in reinventing the wheel. While it is true that self-
devised classroom resources are often the most effective, there is no
point in duplicating projects and programmes which are already
available elsewhere.

Many of the materials listed below were originally developed by
teachers in schools all over the country who needed to enrich and
extend their schemes of work and classroom programmes.

The list is not exhaustive. Chapter 8 listed a number of organisations
which offer their own reading and resource lists and related references.
Books on the teaching of individual subjects often carry useful
bibliographies. One of the authors' own books, *Teaching Mathematics*
by Tom Marjoram, lists a large number of sources useful to
mathematics teachers; another, *Teaching Able Children* by Tom
Marjoram in this same series, carries a substantial bibliography of DES
and other publications, research references and curriculum enrichment
materials for able pupils.

Many of the following suggestions are of a cross-curricular nature.

Berkshire Enrichment Materials
These are published by LDA (Learning Development Aids), at Dept D,
Duke Street, Wisbech, Cambs PE13 2AE and include:

- *The Motorway Project – 9–13 years.*
- *Village of Eddington – 9–13 years.*
- *Townscapes – 9–13 years.*
- *My hand.*
- *Learning through drama.*
- *Inuit.*
- *Go and find out.*

Edward de Bono's material has been used all over the world and includes the *Cort Thinking Program* and six Thinking Lessons on Breadth, Organisation, Interaction, Creativity, Information and Feeling, Actions.

Centre for Creativity, Innovation and Leadership Materials mainly about innovative thinking and leadership are available from the Associate Director Hilda Rosselli, Human Sciences Building 414, University of South Florida, Tampa, FL 33620, USA.

Chip Foundation Ltd A useful Australian contact at School of Education, University of Melbourne, Parkville, Victoria 3052, Australia.

Essex has built up one of the more extensive sets of enrichment materials in recent years. These are the Essex Curriculum Extension Projects available from Dr Julian Whybra, Essex County Advisory Teacher for Gifted Education, Ongar Curriculum Support Centre, Fyfield Road, Chipping Ongar, Essex. They include:

- *The Manor of Wodensfeld optional BBC-B disk*, Stephen Baines, age range (AR) 11–18.
- *An Introductory Study of Some Aspects of Pollution*, John Llewellyn-Jones, AR 13–18.
- *Anglo-Saxon Literature*, Tony Smith, AR 13–18.
- *The Battle of Isandhlwana optional slides*, Julian Whybra, AR 13–18.
- *An Introduction to Genetic Engineering*, Davina Tweddle, AR 13–18.
- *Mediaeval Castle-Building*, Stephen Baines, AR 11–18.
- *The Saxon Settlement of South-East Esssex*, Julian Whybra, AR 11–18.
- *Cunning Passages, Contrived Corridors*, Stephen Baines, AR 13–18.
- *Sounds Appalling*, Pauline Hirst, AR 12–14.
- *A Poor Man's Guide to Genealogy*, Julian Whybra, AR 11–18.
- *May the Force be with You*, Jim Hind, AR 13–18.
- *Ten, Sixty-six, And All That*, Jim Hind, AR 13–18.
- *Some Questions of Energy*, Barry Adams and Pauline Hirst, AR 12–15.
- *Cunning Men, Wise Women*, John Senior, AR 11–18.
- *A Matter of Concentration*, David Stamp, AR 12–14.

- *Problems with Liquids*, Jim Molineaux, AR 12–14.
- *Colour in Rocks and Minerals optional slides*, Neil Cook, AR 12–14.
- *Essex Witchcraft*, Geoff Rees, AR 13–18.
- *Nes'Ammim*, John Wood, AR 13–18.
- *Mediaeval Merchant*, Stephen Baines, AR 11–18.
- *A Knyght Ther Was*, Stephen Baines, AR 11–18.
- *Raindrops upon a Soil Surface*, Steve Rogers, AR 13–18.
- *Beggars on Golden Stools*, Joy Clayworth, AR 13–15.
- *The Sinking of the Lusitania*, David Shannon, AR 13–15.
- *A Question of Sovereignty*, Julian Whybra, AR 11–18.
- *Grimm's Fairy talc?*, Julian Whybra, AR 12–18.
- *Surnames*, Julian Whybra, AR 11–16.
- *Polyominoes*, Julian Whybra, AR 9–15.
- *Palindromic Numbers*, Julian Whybra, AR 9–15.
- *Language Aptitude Test*, various, AR 11–18.
- *Directory Enquiries*, Julian Whybra, AR 11–18.
- *Codebreaking*, Julian Whybra, AR 11–14.
- *The Joe Bailey Situation*, Stephen Baines, AR 11–18.
- *Persecution*, Stephen Baines, AR 11–18.
- *Classical Studies*, Stephen Baines, AR 11–18.
- *Man and Superman*, Julian Whybra, AR 11–18.
- *The Anglo-Saxon Alphabet*, Julian Whybra, AR 9–18.
- *Elizabethan Script*, Julian Whybra, AR 9–18.
- *Wincescumbescire – the place thereof shall know it no more*, Julian Whybra, AR 13–18.
- *Mathematical Structure*, Eric Marson, AR 13–15.
- *Corrosion*, Paul Shiel, AR 12–14.
- *Chromatography*, Davina Tweddle, AR 13–18.
- *Astronomy and the Wave Properties of Light*, Chris Ellis, AR 13–15.
- *An Introduction to Philosophy*, George Warren, AR 13–15.
- *Random Numbers*, Tim Moore, AR 13–15.
- *Water Pollution and Biotic Indexing*, Davina Tweddle, AR 12–14.
- *Crystallography*, Chris Ellis, AR 13–15.
- *Art History Workshop*, Diana Naylor, AR 13–15.
- *Language Decipherment*, Stephen Baines, AR 11–18.
- *A New Capital for Denmark*, Julian Whybra, AR 11–18.
- *Russian times Elizabethan*, Julian Whybra, AR 9–18.
- *Electronics*, S Dando, AR 14–16.
- *Twinkle, Twinkle*, Jim Hind, AR 14–16.
- *A Mathematical Mystery Tour*, Eric Marson, AR 14–16.

- *Nuclear Physics: The Mass Formula*, Jim Hind, AR 12–14.
- *Weather*, Chris Martin, AR 8–12.
- *Maps*, Chris Martin, AR 8–12.
- *Ah-Jon-Jon*, Valerie Webb, AR 8–11.
- *Colour*, various, AR 8–12.
- *Time and Space*, various, AR 8–12.
- *Lego-Genetics*, Susan Baines, AR 5–12.
- *Thirty-six Things to do with a Poem*, various, AR 7–11.
- *Twenty-two Ideas for Variety in Comprehension Work*, various, AR 7–11.
- *Twenty-four Things to do with a Book*, various, AR 7–11.
- *Textures*, Linden Lynn, AR 9–11.
- *Modular Arithmetic*, Dorothy Geering, AR 9–11.
- *Puzzlers*, Eleanor Williams, AR 8–12.
- *Cubes*, Eleanor Williams, AR 8–12.
- *Accounts*, Glennis Rogerson, AR 10–11.
- *Law and Common Sense*, Glennis Rogerson, AR 10–11.
- *A Study of Two East Anglian Islands*, J A Wilson, AR 8–12.
- *Central Place Theory*, Hilary Goodyear, AR 9–11.
- *Six Mathematical Games*, Jim Hind, AR 9–13.
- *How Many?*, Jim Hind, AR 8–12.
- *Test on Following Instructions*, various, AR 8–14.
- *Worksheets in Biology*, Susan Baines, AR 7–13.
- *Plant and Animal Structure*, Belle Wallace, AR 8–11.
- *An Introduction to Ecology*, A Watkinson and P Wells, AR 8–13.
- *Working with Dinosaurs*, Barbara Bexley, AR 5–7.
- *Working with Early Man*, Barbara Bexley, AR 5–7.
- *Working with Snails*, Barbara Bexley, AR 5–7.
- *Working with Air*, Barbara Bexley, AR 5–7.
- *Anglo-Saxon*, Julian Whybra, AR 5–7.
- *Identifying the Gifted Child*, Belle Wallace and John Acklaw.
- *Providing for the Gifted Child*, Belle Wallace and John Acklaw.
- *Provision for Gifted Children in Essex, 1964–1980*, Belle Wallace.
- *Provision for Gifted Children in Essex, 1980–1987*, Julian Whybra.
- *The Gifted Child in School*, Belle Wallace.
- *Is there hope for intelligent life in comprehensive schools?*, Stephen Baines.
- *Impact, Problem-solving*, Stephen Baines.
- *Extra Studies at Philip Morant School*, Stephen Baines.
- *The Gifted Child in the Philip Morant Classroom*, Stephen Baines.
- *Provision for Very Able Children at Mark Hall School*, Alistair Clarke.

- *Able Pupils at Stewards School*, Isobel Urquhart.
- *Extra Studies at Billericay School: Set of Related Forms*, Alistair Brown.
- *Book List for up to 6 year old*, Pat Dixon, AR 4–6.
- *Fifty Books for Infants who are Good Readers*, Pat Dixon, AR 6–8.
- *Suggested Books for Fluent Readers in Primary Schools*, various, AR 8–11.
- *Resources for Teaching Mathematically Able Pupils (Wiltshire CC)*, Anita Straker, AR 9–19.
- *Sources for Mathematical Extension Activities*, W Baldwin, AR 8–18.
- *Science Fiction for Young Readers*, David Pringle, AR 8–13.
- *Simulation Games: Geography*, N Grenyer, AR 7–19.
- *25 Books for A Level History*, John Bald and Marion Dodds, AR 16–18.
- *Annotated List of German Reading Books*, C Weekes and S Morgan, AR 11–14.
- *Sixth-Form Reading in Science*, John Bald and Marion Dadds, AR 16–18.
- *Gifted Education: An Address List*, Julian Whybra.
- *Essex Curriculum Extension Projects*, Julian Whybra.
- *Curriculum Extension and Counselling for More Able Pupils at Rainsford School*, David Proudlock.
- *Mathematics Software for use in Mathematics Lessons*, C Christofides, AR 10–14.

Hampshire Thanks to the activities of Miss E G Bennett, Advisory Teacher for the Gifted at PTRC, Sundridge Close, Cosham, Portsmouth PO6 3JL, this authority produces valuable *Material for the Able Child, MACH*, and also, as part of their Curriculum Differentiation Initiative, the publication 'Matching the Curriculum to the Needs of the Individual'.

Israel has been long associated with research and curriculum development work for talented young people. A recent publication available from the Ministry of Education and Culture, Jerusalem, is entitled *Gifted Children and Science Oriented Youth Information Booklet*.

Another major source of enrichment material, much of it generated in the course of a TRIST project, is available from the headquarters of the **National Association for Curriculum Enrichment and Extension (NACE)** at Nene College, Moulton Park, Northampton NN2 7AL.

The Association's informative newsletter is available from Mrs Maree Jacob Tel: (0604) 710308. Resources available include the following:

1. *Teacher Guidance Booklets on Able Pupils* written by J B Teare.

   (a) 'A School Policy on Provision for Able Pupils'.
   (b) 'Able Pupils: Practical Identification Strategies'.
   (c) 'The Writing of Curriculum Enrichment Materials'.

2. 'From Little Acorns', produced by J B Teare. This pack comprises 13 items:

   - 'Storytails' – a creative writing exercise combining considerable open-endedness with some parameters.
   - 'A Question of Identity' – the investigation of an inheritance claim involves information-processing, logical thought, deduction, problem-solving and role-play.
   - 'Animalerisms' – imaginative thinking about animal behaviour.
   - 'Snakes and Races, Squares and Quotients' – the production of a game board encourages the use of mathematical ideas and language.
   - 'The Magic Number' – a series of connected puzzles is designed to promote the use of mathematical language.
   - 'Exhibit A' – the imaginative use of evidence within a creative writing setting.
   - 'Spot the Difference' – a pictorial code.
   - 'Silhouette' – an item on the theme of vocabulary, involving word play, reference work and classification.
   - 'One Swallow' – plays upon the abstract quality of proverbs.
   - 'Odd One Out' – classification and connections are the important features but the item also encourages research.
   - 'A Matter of Form' – organisation, following instructions and decision-making are involved in a school-based exercise.
   - 'Many Happy Returns' – a logical thought problem in a multicultural setting.
   - 'From Little Acorns' – a standard exercise on family trees extended beyond the normal demands.

3. *Science Materials*

   - *Top Bird*, M Poole.
   - *Tomatoes Galore*, M Poole.

- *Organisms and Environment*, B Molner.
- *Interactive Exercises on Science Topics I*, D R George.

Further science materials by each of the above authors are likely to be available by the beginning of the Spring Term 1991. They are as follows:

- *Alive with Nitrogen*, M Poole.
- *Balance is Life*, M Poole.
- *About Energy*, B Milner.
- *More about Energy*, B Milner.
- *Solving a Current Problem*, B Milner.
- *Interactive Exercises on Science Topics II*, D R George.
- *The Sea*, J A Streaton.

4. *Resources Handbook*

- *Bibliography*
  A selective list of books on the education of very able pupils, for teachers and parents.
- *Mathematics, science and technology*
  Resources in these areas of the curriculum which will extend able children.
- *Puzzles, games and simulations*
  Cross-curricular resources encouraging children to think in a variety of ways.

The **National Council for Educational Technology (NCET)**, Sir W Lyons Road, Science Park, University of Warwick, Coventry CV4 7EZ encourages supported self-study, has a publication, a consultancy and an information service and also produces a termly newsletter.

Newcastle Materials for the More Able 5–7 years

- *Stamps and the Postman.*
- *The Shopping Basket.*
- *Home Sweet Home.*

Projects
One group of teachers have begun to produce their own printed materials and software trading under the name FG Projects. The following projects are available from them at 11 Damask Road, Colchester, Essex.

- *National Park*, AR 13–17.
- *Rivers*, AR 11–18.
- *Conurbation*, AR 13–17.
- *CBD*, AR 13–17.
- *The Development Area Game*, AR 13–17.
- *New Town*, AR 13–17.
- *Geography Exercises Pack*, AR 13–17.
- *Beer (with BBC disk)*, AR 15–18.
- *Water (with BBC disk)*, AR 11–16.
- *Motorway (with BBC disk)*, AR 11–16.
- *An English Village 1851*, AR 11–16.
- *Canal Mania*, AR 13–16.
- *The Darnley Murder*, AR 11–16.
- *The Rail Crash Mystery*, AR 13–16.
- *Norman Dynasty*, AR 9–13.
- *Drake's Voyage (with BBC disk)*, AR 11–16.
- *The Railway Barons (with BBC disk)*, AR 14–18.
- *Victorian Coalminer (with BBC disk)*, AR 11–16.
- *Tudor England (with BBC disk)*, AR 11–16.
- *Poverty Line (with BBC disk)*, AR 13–16.
- *The Workhouse (with BBC disk)*.
- *Power (with BBC disk)*.

One English firm which devotes itself exclusively to producing enrichment and extension material is **Pullen Publications Ltd**, 121 London Road, Knebworth, Herts SG3 6EX. Of particular note are the School Industry Resource Packs on:

- *Superstores and Supermarkets*
- *Wind Energy*
- *North Sea Oil*
- *The Printing Industry*
- *Inspection and Testing Machines*
- *Grasses including Cereals*.

Other publications are:

- *Hedgehoppers for the Young*
- *Fun with Early Maths*
- *Fighting Men*, R Callow
- *Problems for Young Mathematicians*, Dr J Coffman
- *Exploring Graphs*, P Sudworth.

Another Australian journal comes from the **Queensland Association for**

Gifted and Talented Children and is available at PO Box 121, Ashgrove, QLD 4060, Australia. Queensland is the only state in Australia which has a full team of some eight or nine inspectors concentrating upon curriculum extension and enrichment for the talented and able.

Nearer home a surprisingly rich range of challenging study projects with strong industrial overtones have been developed by the **Shell Education Service**, Shell UK Ltd, Shell Mex House, Strand, London WC2R 0DX. These are available from Bankside House, West Mills, Newbury, Berks RG14 5HP, and are listed below. Obtainable too, are 'The Journey to Enterprise' and 'The Shell Interactive Video Project Pack', compatible with BBC and Nimbus IV systems.

L1	*Today's Oil = Tomorrow's Energy* (publication)
W1	*The Oil Story* (wallcharts)
GB2	*Oil* (publication)
EXB9	*The Hidden Resource* (publication)
W2	*Oil Refining* (wallcharts)
EXB10	*Oil Beneath Our Feet* (publication)
W4	*Operation North Sea* (wallcharts)
B1	*Topics from your Tidy Box* (publication)
B2	*Science from your Shopping Basket*
W5	*Molecules from Oil* (wallcharts)
D1	*Molecules from Oil* (deskcharts)
B5	*Petrochemicals* (publication)
P1	*Petrochemicals Pack* (publication)
B10	*Chemicals from Oil* (publication)
B6	*Carbon* (publication)
B4	*Energy* (publication)
W6	*Energy through the Ages* (wallchart)
L2	*Facts about Petrol* (publication)
L3	*Facts about Motor Oils* (publication)
L4	*Facts about Natural Gas* (publication)
L5	*Facts about Coal* (publication)
B7	*Computers at work for Shell* (publication)
W9	*Computers at work for Shell* (wallcharts)
W10	*Learning from Fossils* (wallchart)
D2	*Learning from Fossils* (deskchart)
GB3	*Billiton and non-ferrous metals* (publication)
B15	*Farms to visit in Britain*
W21	*The Farming Year* (wallchart)
W22	*Farming in the UK* (wallchart)

B9	*Chemicals on the Farm* (publication)
W13	*Chemicals on the Farm* (wallchart)
UB1	*Good Neighbours* (publication)
W14	*Biological Cycles* (wallcharts)
W23	*Pond and Woodland Food Webs* (wallcharts)
W12	*Insect Life Histories* (wallcharts)
UB6	*Shell UK Limited Annual Report*
GB17	*The Shell Transport and Trading Company Limited Annual Report*
GB19	*Shell at a Glance*
UB7	*Shell UK Limited*
B11	*Shell's Own Shell*
B12	*'Times Change . . .'*
L7	*Facing the Future*
W15	*Working for Yourself* (wallchart)
D3	*Working for Yourself* (deskchart)
B13	*Catalogue of Resources for Teachers 89/90*
UB8	*Shell Film Catalogue 89/90*

A further, less extensive set of materials and associated courses and seminars are offered by the **Smallpiece Trust**, 27 Newbold Terrace East, Leamington Spa, Warwicks CV32 4ES; tel (0926) 336423. Some of these seminars and courses are held at the Trust's headquarters; others are available on site at the applying school. They are on:

- Computer Aided Design
- Computer Aided Manufacture
- Thinking about Thinking
- Engineering Technology
- Problem-solving for Teachers
- Computer Aided Design for Teachers

An extremely interesting study into the relative performances of girls and boys, giving noteworthy statistics and entitled 'Room for Improvement' is available from the **Tasmanian Education Dept**, North Hobart.

Available in **Tasmania** are packs such as 'From the Ground Up' from the Good Ideas Factory, G and T Resources Centre, Anglesea Street, South Hobart 7004, TAS.

Finally, one major American publisher who specialises in enrichment and extension publications and materials is the **Trillium Press**, PO Box 209, Monroe, NY 10950, USA. Their list includes:

- *Philosophy for Young Thinkers*

- *Cartoons for Thinking*
- *Computer Ethics*
- *The Animal Kingdom*
- *Our Community*
- *A New Way to use your Brain*
- *Suppose the Wolf were an Octopus*
- *Aesop's Fables*
- *Early Childhood Music Kit*
- *Concept Booster*
- *Curtain I and II (Drama)*
- *Brain Booster*
- *Keyboard Banger*
- *Physical Science for Young Children*
- *What Colour is Newton's Apple?*
- *Logo Activity Cards*
- *Creative Encounters*
- *Ancient Greece*
- *Introductory Geometrics*
- *Future Studies*
- *Management Systems for Gifted and Special Education Programmes.*

Trilliam Press director, Tom Kemnitz, takes a vigorous lead in this field of publishing and he has also published many of the voluminous proceedings of World Conferences on Gifted and Talented Children which have been held in London, San Francisco, Jerusalem, Montreal, Manilla, Hamburg, Salt Lake City and Sydney. The next will be in the Hague (29 July–2 August, 1991) and the tenth in Toronto (1993). These conferences have provided and will continue to provide a world stage and forum for research, materials and new teaching ideas in the field.

Finally, here are a few **miscellaneous**, more subject-based resources which are also available and recommended:

Advisory Unit for Comp-Based Education, Edymion Road, Hatfield	Maths
ATM, Kings Chambers, Queen Street, Derby	Maths/Comp
BBC Science Topics, BBC, PO Box 234, London	Chem, Phys, Biol
BP Education Service, Britannic House, Moor Lane, London	Oil/energy
Earosoft Resources Centre, Back Hill, Ely	Maths

Essex Curriculum Extension Project, J Whybra, Meadgate Centre, Mascalls Way, Gt Baddow, Essex	All subject areas
F G Projects, 11 Damask Road, Colchester	Hist, Geog
Ginn & Co, Prebendal House, Parson's Fee, Aylesbury, Bucks HP20 2QZ	Comp in various
P Huxtable Designs, Freepost, Worcester WR6 5BR	CDT
Ilea English Centre, NATE, 49 Broomgrove Road, Sheffield	English
Lancaster PAC, PO Box 61, County Hall, Preston	Prim, Hum, Maths
LDA Duke Street, Wisbech	Prim, Hum
Longfield Press, 6 Longfield Gardens, Tring	Maths
Math Association, 259 London Road, Leicester	Maths
MEP SMILE, 275 Kennington Lane, London	Maths
MFA Unilab Limited, Clarendon Road, Blackburn	Electronics
NACE, Nene College, Moulton Park, Northampton NN2 7AL	Science
Pentangle Puzzles, Over Wallop, Hants	Games
RLDU, Bishop Road, Bishopston, Bristol	Prim Hums
Royal Institution, 21 Albermarle Street, London	Maths, Masterclasses
Shell Centre, University of Nottingham	Maths, Music
Spode Group, Cranfield Inst of Tech, Bedford	Maths
SRA Ltd, Newtown Road, Henley-on-Thames	Prim Hums
Tarquin Publics, Stradbroke, Diss.	Maths
J B Teare, The King's School, Ottery St Mary, Devon	Problem-solving
Tressell Publications, 70 Grand Parade, Brighton	Hist/Maths
UKAEA, Education Service, ITRC, PO Box 10, Wetherby	Phys/Comp

Bibliography

ATM (1964) *Some Lessons in Mathematics* (ed T J Taylor) CUP

ATM (1984) *Teaching Styles in Mathematics: A Response to Cockcroft 243* ATM

Albert, RS (1983) *Genius and Eminence: The Social Psychology of Creativity and Exceptional Achievement* Pergamon Press

Association of British Chambers of Commerce (1984) *Business and the School Curriculum* ABCC

Ball, F (1977) *The Development of Reading Skills: A Book of Resources for Teachers* Blackwell

Barbe, W B and Renzulli, J S (1975) *Psychology and Education of the Gifted* J Wiley

Barnes, D (1982) *Practical Curriculum Study* Routledge & Kegan Paul

Barrass, R (1982) *Students Must Write: A Guide to Better Writing in Course Work and Examinations* Methuen

Bennett, N, Desforges, A, Cockburn, A and Wilkinson, B (1984) *The Quality of Pupils' Learning Experiences* Lawrence Erlbaum Associates Ltd

Biggs, E (1983) *Confident Mathematics Teaching 5-13* NFER-Nelson

Bird, M (1983) *Generating Mathematical Activity in the Classroom* West Sussex IHE

Brierley, J (1973) *The Thinking Machine* Heinemann

Bruner, J (1966) *Towards a Theory of Instruction* Harvard

Burton (1984) *Thinking Things Through* Blackwell

Calderwood, J (1984) *Teachers' Classroom Decision Making* Holt Rinehart & Winston

Cofman, J (1981) *Problems for Young Mathematicians* Pullen Publications

Cornelius, M (ed) (1982) *Teaching in Mathematics* Croom Helm

Cox, J, Daniel, N and Boston, B (1985) *Educating Able Learners* University of Texas Press

Craft, A and Bardell, G (eds) (1984) *Curriculum Opportunities in a Multicultural Society* Harper & Row

Crawford, D H (1975) *The Fife Mathematics Project: An Experiment in Individual Learning* OUP

Cunningham, P (1988) *Curriculum Change in the Primary School since 1945*, Falmer

Davies, I K (1971) *The Management of Learning* McGraw Hill

DES (1981) *The Contribution of Craft, Design and Technology to the Teaching of Mathematics* HMSO

Davies, Z P (1973) *Mathematics Through the Senses, Games, Dance and Art* NFER–Nelson

Dearden, R F (1984) *Theory and Practice in Education* Routledge & Kegan Paul

Deem, Rosemary, The Great Education Reform Bill in *Education Policy* Vol 3, No 2

Denton, C and Postlethwaite, K (1985) *Able Children* NFER–Nelson

J Denyer for Schools Council (1983) *Mathematics Across the Curriculum* Longman

Dunstan, J (1978) *Paths to Excellence and the Soviet School* NFER–Nelson

Eggleston, J (ed) (1980) *Schools-based Curriculum Development in Britain: A Collection of Case Studies* Routledge & Kegan Paul

Eggleston, J (1979) *Teacher Decision Making in the Classroom* Routledge & Kegan Paul

Essex C C Education Department (1976) *The Mathematical Requirements of Industry: An Interim Report* Essex Education Department

Fowler, W R (1990) *Implementing the National Curriculum* Kogan Page

Fowler, W R (1988) *Towards the National Curriculum* Kogan Page

Freeman, J (ed) (1985) *The Psychology of Gifted Children* Wiley

Galton, M (ed) (1978) *British Mirrors: A Collection of Classroom Observation Systems* University of Leicester, School of Education

Galton, M (ed) (1980) *Curriculum Change: Lessons of a Decade* The Leicester University Press

Galton, M and Moon, R (eds) (1983) *Changing School, Changing Curriculum* Harper & Row

George, W C (1979) *Educating the Gifted: Acceleration and Enrichment* Johns Hopkins University Press

Getzels, J W and Jackson, P W (1968) *Creativity and Intelligence* Wiley

Gordon, P (ed) (1981) *The Study of the Curriculum* Batsford Academic and Educational

Gowan, J C and Torrance, E P (1971) *Education of the Ablest*, Peacock Publications

Grellet, F (1981) *Developing Reading Skills* CUP
Grenyer, N (1983) *Geography for Gifted Pupils* Longman
Grubb, D H W (ed) (1982) *The Gifted Child at School: A Review of Current Theory and Practice* Oxford Society for Applied Studies in Education
Haggitt, E M (1975) *Projects in the Primary School* Longman
Hahn, R O (1973) *Creative Teachers: Who Wants Them?* Wiley (USA)
Hamblin, D (1981) *Teaching Study Skills* Basil Blackwell
Harri-Augstein, S et al (1982) *Reading to Learn* Methuen
Hart, D and Russell, U (1988) *The Education Reform Act 1988 Booklet and Video* BBC Education with the Industrial Society
Hemmings, J (1981) *The Betrayal of Youth* Open Forum Series
Hirst, P H (1968) *Changing the Curriculum* University of London Press
Hirst, P (1984) *Knowledge and the Curriculum* Routledge & Kegan Paul
Hoare, R J (1971) *Topic Work with Books* G Chapman
Holt, J (1970) *The Underachieving School* Pitman
Horton, T and Raggett, P (eds) (1982) *Challenge and Change in the Curriculum: A reader for the Purpose and Planning in the Curriculum course at O U* Hodder and Stoughton with the Open University
Howson, G (1981) *Curriculum Development in Mathematics* CUP
ILEA (1985) *Improving Primary Schools: Report of the Committee on Primary Education* (Chairman Mr N Thomas, CBE)
ILEA (1984) *Improving Secondary Schools: Report on the Committee on the Curriculum and Organisation of Secondary Schools* (Chairman Dr D H Hargreaves)
ILEA (1984) *Integrated Studies and the Humanities in the Lower Secondary School: A discussion Paper* ILEA
Irvin, A (ed) (1982) *Starting to Teach Study Skills* Edward Arnold
Johnson, D C (1983) *Explore Maths with your Micro: A Book for Kids aged 9 to 90* Heinemann Computers in Education Ltd
Kastner, B (1978) *Applications of Secondary School Mathematics* NCTM
Kelly, A V (1982) *The Curriculum: Theory and Practice* (2nd edn), Harper & Row
Kerry, T (1982) *Effective Questioning: A Teaching Skills Workbook* Macmillan Education
Kerry, T (1981) *Teaching Bright Pupils in Mixed Ability Classes: A Self-instructional Handbook of Strategies and Suggestions* Macmillan Education
Kerry, T and Sands, M (1982) *Handling Classroom Groups: A Teaching Skills Workbook* Macmillan Education

Kohl, H R (1977) *Writing, Maths and Games in the Open Classroom* Methuen

Kruteskii, V A (1976) *The Psychology of Mathematical Abilities in School Children* University of Chicago Press

Lane, S M and Kemp, M (1973) *An Approach to Topic Work in the Primary School* Blackie

Lawton, D (1980) *The Politics of the School Curriculum* Routledge & Kegan Paul

Lawton, D (1984) *The Tightening Grip: Growth of Central Control of the School Curriculum* Bedford Way Papers 21, London: University of London, Institute of Education

Leyden, S (1985) *Helping the Child of Exceptional Ability* Croom Helm

John Ling for Schools Council (1979) *Mathematics Across the Curriculum* Blackie

Lunzer, E and Gardener, K (1979) *The Effective Use of Reading* Heinemann Educational

Maclure, S (1988) *Education Reformed: A Guide to the Education Reform Act 1988* Hodder & Stoughton

McPeck, P (1981) *Critical Thinking and Education* Martin Robertson

Maingay, S (1983) *Making Sense of Reading* Harrap

Maker, J (1982) *Curriculum Development for the Gifted* Aspen Publications

Maltby, F (1984) *Gifted Children and Teachers in the Primary School* Falmer Press

Marjoram, D T E (1988) *Teaching Able Children* Kogan Page

Marjoram, D T E (1974) *Teaching Mathematics* Heinemann Educational

Marjoram, D T E and Holt, M (1973) *Maths in a Changing World* Heinemann Educational

Marland, M (1975) *The Craft of the Classroom* Heinemann Educational

Martin, L, *The 1988 Education Act: A Tactical Guide for Schools* Blackwell

Math Gazette (1979) *Topics in Mathematics: Ideas for the Secondary Classroom* Bell and Hyman

Milroy, E (1982) *Role-play: A Practical Guide* Aberdeen University Press

Moltershead, L (1985) *Investigations in Mathematics* Blackwell

Nash, R (1973) *Classrooms Observed* Routledge & Kegan Paul

National Association of Headteachers (1989) *Guide to the Education Reform Act 1988* NAHT with Longmans

Nicholls, S H and Nicholls A (1975) *Creative Teaching: An Approach to the Achievement of Educational Objectives* Allen & Unwin

Ogilvie, E (1973) *Gifted Children in Primary Schools* Macmillan Educational

Peters, R S (1966) *Ethics and Education* Allen & Unwin

Pluckrose, H and Wilby, P (eds) (1980) *Education 2000* Maurice Temple Smith

Potts, J (1976) *Beyond Initial Reading* Allen & Unwin

Prosser, P (1981) *The World on Your Doorstep: The Teacher, The Environment and Integrated Studies* McGraw-Hill

Raggett, M and Clarkson, M (1974) *English and Integrated Arts* Ward Lock Educational

Rance, P (1968) *Teaching by Topics* Ward Lock Educational

Renzulli, J S (1977) *The Enrichment Triad Model* Creative Learning Press Inc

Richards, C (1984) *Curriculum Studies: An Introductory Annotated Biography* (2nd edn), Falmer Press

Ruth, B (1977) *Teaching Home Economics in the Integrated Curriculum* Heinemann Educational

Schools Council (1981) *Information Skills in the Secondary Curriculum* (Curriculum Bulletin 9), Methuen Educational

Simkin, D and Simkin, J (1984) *Curriculum Development in Action: Fresh Approaches in the Humanities* Tressell Publications

Skilbeck, M (1984) *School-based Curriculum Development* Harper & Row

Smith, A D (1988) *Starting to Teach* Kogan Page

Smith, P (1983) *Reading Skills and Reference Work* Macmillan Educational

Spode Group (1982) *Solving Real Problems with Mathematics* Cranfield Institute of Technology Press

Stanley, J C et al (1974) *Mathematical Talent: Discovery, Description and Development* Johns Hopkins University Press

Stenhouse, L (1983) *Authority, Education and Emancipation* Heinemann Educational

Stevens, A (1981) *Clever Children in Comprehensive Schools* Penguin

Anita Straker for Schools Council (1983) *Mathematics for Gifted Pupils* Longman

Tabberer, R and Allman, J (1981) *Study Skills at 16+: An Interim Report* (NFER Research in Progress 4)

Tannenbaum, A J (1983) *Gifted Children* Macmillan

UKRA Conference (1982) *Reading through the Curriculum* Heinemann Educational

Vygotsky, L S (1962) *Thought and Language* John Wiley and Sons

Walker, C (1974) *Reading Development and Extension* Ward Lock Educational

Wallace, B (1983) *Teaching the Very Able Child* Ward Lock Educational

Waterhouse, P (1983) *Managing the Learning Process* McGraw Hill

White, R (1985) *The 14–18 Curriculum: Integrating CPVE, YTC, TVEI? A Discussion Document* (2nd edn), Bristol Youth Education Service

Whitty, G (1985) *Sociology and School Knowledge* Methuen

Whyte, J (1983) *Sexism in the Secondary Curriculum* Harper & Row

Wilcox, B et al (1984) *The Preparation for Life Curriculum* Croom Helm

Williams, M (1976) *Geography and the Integrated Curriculum: A Reader* Heinemann Educational

Willings, D (1981) *The Creatively Gifted* Woodhead Faulkener

Wilson, E (1983) *The Thoughtful Reader in the Primary School* Hodder & Stoughton

Wollach, M A and Kogan, N (1985) *Models of Thinking in Young Children* Holt, Rinehart & Winston

Woodhouse, J (1987) *The Changing Primary School* Falmer Press

World Council for Gifted Children Conference Proceedings for:

London	1975
San Francisco	1977
Jerusalem	1979
Montreal	1981
Manila	1983
Hamburg	1985
Salt Lake City	1987
Sydney	1989

All available from Trillium Press, New York

Wragg, E C (1981) *Class Management and Control: A Teaching Skills Workbook* MacMillan Education

Further Reading

This chapter lists the foregoing alphabetical selection of relevant texts for study under specialist headings.

The Education Reform Act 1988

Fowler, W R, *Towards the National Curriculum*, Kogan Page (1988).
Fowler, W R, *Implementing the National Curriculum*, Kogan Page (1990).
Hart, D and Russell, U, *The Education Reform Act 1988 Booklet and Video*, BBC Education with the Industrial Society (1988).
Maclure, S, *Education Re-formed: A Guide to the Education Reform Act 1988*, Hodder and Stoughton (1988).
Martin, L, *The 1988 Education Act: A Tactical Guide for Schools*, Blackwell (1988).
National Association of Headteachers, *Guide to the Education Reform Act 1988*, NAHT with Longmans (1989).
Deem, Rosemary, *The Great Education Reform Bill in Education Policy*, Journal of Educational Policy Vol 3, No 2.

Curriculum (general)

Here again, there are many DES publications on curriculum generally, including the 'Curriculum Matters' series. Lists of these are obtainable from Elizabeth House. Other publications include:

Association of British Chambers of Commerce, *Business and the School Curriculum*, ABCC (1984).
Barnes, D, *Practical Curriculum Study*, Routledge & Kegan Paul (1982).
Bruner, J, *Towards a Theory of Instruction* Harvard, (1966).
Craft, A and Bardell, G (eds) *Curriculum Opportunities in a Multicultural Society*, Harper and Row (1984).
Cunningham, P, *Curriculum Change in the Primary School since 1945*, Falmer (1988).

Dearden, R F, *Theory and Practice in Education*, Routledge & Kegan Paul (1984).

Eggleston, J (ed), *Schools-based Curriculum Development in Britain, A Collection of Case Studies*, Routledge & Kegan Paul (1980).

Galton, M (ed), *Curriculum Change: The Lessons of a Decade*, Leicester University Press (1980).

Galton, M and Moon, R (eds), *Changing School . . . Changing Curriculum*, Harper and Row (1983).

Gordon, P (ed), *The Study of the Curriculum*, Batsford Academic and Educational (1981).

Hirst, P H, *Changing the Curriculum*, University of London Press (1968).

Hirst, P, *Knowledge and the Curriculum*, Routledge & Kegan Paul (1984).

Horton, T and Raggett, P (eds), *Challenge and Change in the Curriculum: A Reader for the 'Purpose and Planning in the Curriculum' course at OU*, Hodder and Stoughton with the Open University (1982).

Kelly, A V, *The Curriculum: Theory and Practice* (2nd edn), Harper and Row (1982).

Lawton, D, *The Tightening Grip: Growth of Central Control of the School Curriculum* (Bedford Way Papers 21), ULIE (1984).

Peters, R S, *Ethics and Education* Allen & Unwin (1966).

Pluckrose, H and Wilby, P (eds), *Education 2000*, Maurice Temple Smith (1980).

Richards, C (ed), *Curriculum Studies: An Introductory Annotated Biography* (2nd edn), Falmer Press (1984).

Simkin, D and Simkin, J (eds), *Curriculum Development in Action: Fresh Approaches in the Humanities*, Tressell Publications (1984).

Skilbeck, M, *School-based Curriculum Development*, Harper and Row (1984).

Stenhouse, L, *Authority, Education and Emancipation*, Heinemann Educational Books (1983).

Whitty, G, *Sociology and School Knowledge*, Methuen (1985).

Woodhouse, J, *The Changing Primary School*, Falmer (1987).

Curriculum (primary)

ILEA, *Improving Primary Schools: Report of the Committee on Primary Education* (1985). (Chairman Mr N Thomas, CBE)

Curriculum (secondary)

ILEA, *Improving Secondary Schools: Report on the Committee on the Curriculum and Organisation of Secondary Schools*, (1984). (Chairman Dr DH Hargreaves)

Lawton, D, *The Politics of the School Curriculum*, Routledge & Kegan Paul (1980).

White, R, *The 14–18 Curriculum: Integrating CPVE, YTC, TVEI? A Discussion Document* (2nd edn), (1985)

Whyte, J (ed), *Sexism in the Secondary Curriculum*, Harper and Row (1983).
Wilcox, B et al, *The Preparation for Life Curriculum*, Croom Helm (1984).

Study skills

Barrass, R, *Students Must Write: A Guide to Better Writing in Course Work and Examinations*, Methuen (1982).
Hamblin, D, *Teaching Study Skills*, Basil Blackwell (1981).
Harri-Augstein, S et al, *Reading to Learn*, Methuen (1982).
Irvin, A (ed), *Starting to Teach Study Skills*, Edward Arnold (1982).
McPeck, P, *Critical Thinking and Education*, Martin Robertson (1981).
Schools Council, *Information Skills in the Secondary Curriculum (Curriculum Bulletin 9), Methuen Educational (1981)*.
Tabberer, R and Allman, J, *Study Skills at 16+: An Interim Report (NFER Research in Progress 4)*, NFER (1981)

Integrated studies

ILEA, *Integrated Studies and the Humanities in the Lower Secondary School: A Discussion Paper*, ILEA (1984).
Prosser, P, *The World on Your Doorstep: The Teacher, the Environment, and Integrated Studies*, McGraw-Hill (1982).
Raggett, M and Clarkson, M (ed), *English and Integrated Arts*, Ward Lock Educational (1974).
Ruth, B, *Teaching Home Economics in the Integrated Curriculum*, Heinemann Educational (1977).
Williams, M, *Geography and the Integrated Curriculum: A Reader*, Heinemann Educational (1976).

Teaching method

Calderwood, J, *Teachers' Classroom Decision Making*, Holt Rinehart and Winston (1971).
Davies, I K, *The Management of Learning*, McGraw Hill (1971).
Eggleston, J, *Teacher Decision Making in the Classroom*, Routledge & Kegan Paul (1979).
Galton, M (ed), *British Mirrors: A Collection of Classroom Observation Systems*, University of Leicester School of Education (1978).
Hahn, R O, *Creative Teachers: Who Wants Them?*, Wiley (USA) (1973).
Holt, J, *The Underachieving School*, Pitman (1970).
Kerry, T, *Effective Questioning: A Teaching Skills Workbook*, MacMillan Education (1982).
Kerry, T and Sands, M, *Handling Classroom Groups: A Teaching Skills Workbook*, Macmillan Education (1982).
Marland, M, *The Craft of the Classroom*, Heinemann Educational Books (1975).

Milroy, E, *Role-play: A Practical Guide*, Aberdeen University Press (1982).

Nicholls, S H and Nicholls, A, *Creative Teaching: An Approach to the Achievement of Educational Objectives*, Allen and Unwin (1975).

Rance, P, *Teaching by Topics*, Ward Lock Educational (1968).

Smith, A D, *Starting to Teach*, Kogan Page (1988).

Waterhouse, P, *Managing the Learning Process*, McGraw Hill (1983).

Wragg, E C, *Class Management and Control: A Teaching Skills Workbook*, Macmillan Education (1981).

Primary

Haggitt, E M, *Projects in the Primary School*, Longman (1975).

Hoare, R J, *Topic Work with Books*, G Chapman (1971).

Lane, S M and Kemp, M, *An Approach to Topic Work in the Primary School*, Blackie (1973).

Reading

Ball, F, *The Development of Reading Skills: A Book of Resources for Teachers*, Blackwell (1977).

Grellet, F, *Developing Reading Skills*, CUP (1981).

Lunzer, E and Gardner, K (ed), *The Effective Use of Reading*, Heinemann Educational (1979).

Maingay, S, *Making Sense of Reading*, Harrap (1983).

Potts, J, *Beyond Initial Reading*, Allen and Unwin (1976).

Smith, P, *Reading Skills and Reference Work*, Macmillan Education (1983).

UKRA Conference, *Reading through the Curriculum*, Heinemann Educational (1982).

Walker, C, *Reading Development and Extension*, Ward Lock Educational (1974).

Wilson, E, *The Thoughtful Reader in the Primary School*, Hodder and Stoughton (1983).

Mathematics and mathematical teaching

The previous sections on study skills and reading clearly relate to extending and enriching the curriculum since these are major means of achieving this. In the authors' view, mathematical thinking is also essential to extension and enrichment in every subject in the sense that literacy and numeracy are now basic to in-depth work and communication in all subjects.

The DES has published many documents on mathematics from the APU surveys of mathematical ability through the Cockcroft Report to the 'Curriculum Matters' documents. These are well known, listed elsewhere and so are not recorded here. The emphasis in the following volumes is on extension, cross-curricular aspects and applications of the subject.

ATM, *Some Lessons in Mathematics* (ed TJ Fletcher) (1964).
ATM, *Teaching Styles in Mathematics: A Response to Cockcroft 243* (1984).
Biggs, E, *Confident Mathematics Teaching 5–13*, NFER-Nelson (1983).
Bird, M, *Generating Mathematical Activity in the Classroom*, West Sussex IHE (1983).
Burton, Leonne, *Thinking Things Through*, Blackwell (1984).
Cofman, J, *Problems for Young Mathematicians*, Pullen Publications (1981).
Cornelius, M (ed), *Teaching in Mathematics*, Croom Helm (1982).
Crawford, D H, *The Fife Mathematics Project: An Experiment in Individual Learning*, OUP (1975).
DES, *The Contribution of Craft, Design and Technology to the Teaching of Mathematics*, DES (1981).
Howson, G, *Curriculum Development in Mathematics*, CUP (1981).
Johnson, D C, *Explore Maths with your Micro: A Book for Kids aged 9 to 90*, Heinemann Computers in Education Ltd (1983).
Kastner, B, *Applications of Secondary School Mathematics*, NCTM (1978).
Kohl, H R, *Writing, Maths and Games in the Open Classroom*, Methuen (1977).
Marjoram, D T E, *Teaching Mathematics*, Heinemann Educational (1974).
Marjoram, D T E and Holt, M, *Maths in a Changing World*, Heinemann Educational (1973).
Math Gazette, *Topics in Mathematics: Ideas for the Secondary Classroom*, Bell and Hyman (1979).

The Mathematical Association has its own full list of publications, teaching aids and accessories obtainable from 259 London Road, Leicester LE2 3BE.

J Denyer for Schools Council, *Mathematics Across the Curriculum*, Longman (1983).
Anita Straker for Schools Council, *Mathematics for Gifted Pupils*, Longman (1983).
John Ling for Schools Council, *Mathematics Across the Curriculum*, Blackie (1979).
Moltershead, Lorraine, *Investigations in Mathematics*, Blackwell (1985).
Spode Group, *Solving Real Problems with Mathematics*, Cranfield Institute of Technology Press (1982).

OTHERS
Davies, Z P, *Mathematics Through the Senses, Games, Dance and Art*, NFER (1973).
Essex CC Education Department, *The Mathematical Requirements of Industry: An Interim Report*, Essex Education Department (1976).
Kruteskii, V A, *The Psychology of Mathematical Abilities in School Children*, University of Chicago Press (1976).
Stanley, J C et al, *Mathematical Talent: Discovery, Description and Development*, Johns Hopkins University Press (1974).

Gifted children

It is not only the gifted child who needs occasional enrichment, stimulus, spur or support. There may also be some gifted children who progress rapidly through the levels of the National Curriculum without too much diversion on the way. However, the literature about the very able and talented has pioneered the notions of curriculum enrichment and extension. Indeed, the National Association for Curriculum Enrichment and Extension (NACE) was formed out of the teacher working groups which contributed so much to the Schools Council Third Gifted Children Project. A selection from that literature is therefore relevant here.

FOR SCHOOLS AND LEAS
Grubb, D H W (ed), *The Gifted Child at School: A Review of Current Theory and Practice*, Oxford Society for Applied Studies in Education (1982).
Grenyer, N, *Geography for Gifted Pupils*, Longman (1983).
Kerry, T, *Teaching Bright Pupils in Mixed Ability Classes: A Self-instructional Handbook of Strategies and Suggestions*, Macmillan Education (1981).
Maltby, F, *Gifted Children and Teachers in the Primary School*, Falmer Press (1984).
Marjoram, D T E, *Teaching Able Children*, Kogan Page (1988).
Nash, R, *Classrooms Observed*, Routledge & Kegan Paul (1973).
Ogilvie, E, *Gifted Children in Primary Schools*, Macmillan Education (1973).
Pluckrose, H, *Education 2000* (Chap 4: 'Able Children and Comprehensives'), Maurice Temple Smith (1980).
Stevens, A, *Clever Children in Comprehensive Schools*, Penguin (1981).
Straker, A, *Mathematics for Gifted Pupils*, Longman (1983).
Wallace, B, *Teaching the Very Able Child*, Ward Lock Educational (1983).

GENERAL READERSHIP
Brierley, J, *The Thinking Machine*, Heinemann (1973).
Cox, J, Daniel, N and Boston, B, *Educating Able Learners*, University of Texas Press (1985).
Dunstan, J, *Paths to Excellence and The Soviet School*, NFER (1978).
Freeman, J (ed), *The Psychology of Gifted Children*, Wiley (1985).
Gower and Torrance, *Education of the Ablest*, Peacock Publications
Hemmings, J, *The Betrayal of Youth*, (1981) Open Forum Series.
Leyden, S, *Helping the Child of Exceptional Ability*, Croom Helm (1985).

RESEARCH
Albert, R S, *Genius and Eminence: The Social Psychology of Creativity and Exceptional Achievement*, Pergamon Press (1983).
Barbe, W B and Renzulli, J S, *Psychology and Education of the Gifted*, J Wiley (1975).
Bennett, N, Desforges, A, Cockburn, A and Wilkinson, B, *The Quality of Pupils' Learning Experiences*, Lawrence Erlbaum Associates Ltd (1984).

Denton, C and Postlethwaite, K, *Able Children*, NFER-Nelson (1985).

George, W C, *Educating the Gifted: Acceleration and Enrichment*, Johns Hopkins University Press (1979).

Getzels, J W and Jackson, P W, *Creativity and Intelligence*, Wiley (1968).

Kruteskii, V A, *The Psychology of Mathematical Abilities in School Children*, University of Chicago Press (1976).

Maker, J, *Curriculum Development for the Gifted*, Aspen Publications (1982).

Renzulli, J S, *The Enrichment Triad Model*, Creative Learning Press Inc (1977).

Tannenbaum, A J, *Gifted Children*, Macmillan (1983).

Vygotsky, L S, *Thought and Language*, John Wiley and Sons (1962).

Wollach, M A and Kogan, N, *Models of Thinking in Young Children*, Holt, Rinehart and Winston (1965).

Willings, D, *The Creatively Gifted*, Woodhead Faulkener (1981).

World Council for Gifted Children Conference Proceedings for:

London	1975
San Francisco	1977
Jerusalem	1979
Montreal	1981
Manila	1983
Hamburg	1985
Salt Lake City	1987
Sydney	1989

All available from Trillium Press, New York.

Index